SUSTAINABILITY SUTRA

An Ecological Investigation

Roy Morrison

SelectBooks, Inc.
New York

This edition published by SelectBooks, Inc.
For information address SelectBooks, Inc., New York, New York.

First Edition

ISBN 978-1-59079-387-9

Library of Congress Cataloging-in-Publication Data

Names: Morrison, Roy, author.
Title: Sustainability sutra : an ecological investigation / Roy Morrison.
Description: First edition. | New York : SelectBooks, Inc., [2017] | Includes
  bibliographical references and index.
Identifiers: LCCN 2015040049 | ISBN 9781590793879 (pbk. : alk. paper)
Subjects: LCSH: Environmentalism. | Sustainable development.
Classification: LCC GE195 .M6653 2017 | DDC 338.9/27--dc23 LC record
available at http://lccn.loc.gov/2015040049

Book design by Janice Benight

Manufactured in the United States of America
10 9 8 7 6 5 4 3 2 1

Sustainability Sutra is the first title in our new line of Sustainability Now books

W elcome to the SelectBooks line of Sustainability Now books. This series of books will draw together a variety of voices with a single purpose—creating a sustainable future for our planet through increasing public awareness about the existential threat to our species.

In order to navigate this multifaceted and frequently misunderstood subject, the publisher has recruited an advisory panel of important leaders across multiple disciplines to lend their perspective and insight. This panel includes:

ERVIN LASZLO – internationally esteemed philosopher of science, systems theorist, Founder and President of the Club of Budapest, and author of numerous books and articles, including *You Can Change the World*

SCOTT JACKSON – civil rights activist, philanthropist, President and CEO of Global Impact

BILL GLADSTONE – author, filmmaker, producer of *Tapping the Source*, Founder and President of Waterside Productions

In our current lives we face daily reports of the destructive levels of carbon emissions and deforestation on our earth and are warned of the damage to our bodies from thousands of petrochemicals in our food supply and household products. It's easy to see how the human behavior that causes these threats to our ecology cannot go on. But what can we do about it? SelectBooks hopes that the Sustainability Now publications will provide you with some of the knowledge and inspiration to take action on the most critical issues confronting humankind.

It is our firm conviction that the only way for us to get past this extreme danger is for all of us to join together and do our part. The Sustainability Now series is calling on you to join the effort.

For Luanne Atsina Baker, my wife,
who has helped shape my work and made this book possible
&
Samuel Schaffer-Morrison, my son,
who is studying conservation biology

Contents

. . . who knows the sutras knows it to be thus.

FROM THE VAYU PURANA

~

We're not our skin of grime, we're not dread bleak
dusty imageless locomotives, we're golden sunflowers
inside, blessed by our own seed & hairy naked
accomplishment-bodies growing into mad black formal
sunflowers in the sunset, spied on by our own eyes
under the shadow of the mad locomotive riverbank
sunset Frisco hilly tincan evening sitdown vision.

ALLEN GINSBURG, "SUNFLOWER SUTRA"

~

Thus shall you think of all this fleeting world:
A star at dawn, a bubble in a stream;
A flash of lightening in a summer cloud,
A flickering lamp, a phantom, and a dream.

DIAMOND SUTRA

Foreword

by *Michael Charles Tobias, PhD*
President, Dancing Star Foundation

The word "sustainability" has been more abused by common misconstrual—dating to the earliest notions of human supremacy over all other species—than even the word "love," which at least we most often apply to one another with, at times, meaningful intimations.

Indeed I have recently heard it more and more repeated that "sustainability" is meaningless, based upon the pervasive social inertia, political apathy, environmental and animal rights activists' depression, conservation biology burn-out, increasing economic gaps between haves and have-nots, and underlying realizations in so many guises that "to have" in the Anthropocene (*anthropo* for man and *cene* for new) is the worst illusion of all, for those relatively few members of our species that is solely responsible for this Sixth Massive Extinction Spasm in the annals of biology.

The sixth great mass extinction event now underway, referred to as the Anthropocene Extinction, marks our predatory civilization with Holocaust-indexes, preparing future historians for the likely possibility that they will not even exist—that history itself, as documented in human terms, will cease altogether.

Roy Morrison, early on in his startling manifesto *Sustainability Sutra,* invokes the memory of "the earliest known placental mammal, our shrew-like ancestor. *Juramaia sinensis*, says Morrison, "lived amidst the dinosaurs 165 million years ago in what is now Northeast China." For the last 60 or so million years, hominid and avifauna evolution have surfaced in ways ripe with perfected equanimity amid flux of every conceivable nuance. Invertebrate populations have not had the advantage of computational biological study because stochastic predictions have dominated mathematical approaches to the eco-sciences, leaving out the gaps that cannot, in real time, be understood. This is a crucial corollary to any ethic that might be aspired to in reaching toward a short, near, and long-term solution for the human dilemma we—each of us—has contributed to, in what can best be characterized as a grave and irreversible calamity for the rest of life on Earth.

Morrison has achieved a beatific unthinkable in evoking the wisdom of both John Ruskin's four political essays of his *Unto This Last*, and Aldo Leopold's *Sand County Almanac: And Sketches Here and There*. By that lyrical and Talmudic-like juxtaposition, we have in this one digestible series of progressive insights a magnificently lit cartography for saving the world. Quite literally, Morrison has given consumers, legislators, poets and scientists, and educators and world leaders a "guide to the perplexed." It could not have emerged at a more terrifying moment in the short biological history of our species. We are in serious trouble, and that crisis is the currently documented holistic collapse of over 44,000 populations of organisms every day and the likelihood that thousands of species are going extinct every day, if one takes into consideration the fact that there are not 1.8 million, 5 million, or 10 million species on Earth. But there are more likely 100 million when taking into account the ever-debated taxonomy of bacteria, archaea, protista, and fungi, not to mention the virtually unknown proliferation of viral species.

The numbers game reflects a large moral quandary: How can one species be empowered by its own consciousness to inflict the biological equivalent of an asteroid inducing, overnight, a global extinction event? For that is what is now occurring, not in astro-geophyscial time, but in biological time. In other words, this is measurable by seconds, minutes, and hours.

The power vested in this calamity belongs to one organism, currently numbering approximately 7.3+ billion ungainly bipedal largely carnivorous *Homo sapiens*, soon to become 9.5, 10, 11, possibly 12 billion in number. Our seemingly unfazed rapacity roars like a train barreling through a dark tunnel in the night, its headlights turned inward. We are out of control and engendering Holocausts in every direction, day by day.

Economists and politicians are held largely accountable for this destruction, while each of us knows full well that we cooperate willingly by our also accountable consumptive practices and relative indifference to distance and time, as measured by geographical and humanly perceived gaps in logic. The logic that Roy Morrison brings to the table in this remarkable work of art and thinking should overturn the complacency that has caused our present downfalls, giving deliverance to those believers in our ability as a species to reverse our pernicious self-importance.

Morrison does more than simply apply his logic by citing salient examples along the way. He activates an applied ethics, as the phrase has more and more come of age, in a manner befitting the sheer complexity of multi-nefarious complicities.

As we recently held the UN Climate Change Conference in Paris in late 2015, and as more and more large vertebrates (those weighing over 100 kilograms) become extinct, the timing for this publication could not be more critical and significant. Should we fail to heed the science and poetry herein—a poetic not unlike what was first intoned by Erasmus Darwin in the late 18th century (Charles Darwin's grandfather)—then, I fear, and I say this with all sincerity and urgency, that we will fail to do what is necessary to configure some level of salvation for the majority of life. Nothing less is at stake.

Morrison has created a masterful work at a moment unprecedented in the history of previously collapsed civilizations. His honesty is potent—his message as breathlessly graphic as those early engravings on copper by Martin Schongauer and his successor,

Albrecht Dürer, that told of the Passion of Christ, the Temptation of St. Anthony as he was being hurled to Earth by demons, or the phenomenal "Vision of St. Eustace" by Pisanello that hangs in London's National Gallery, in which the Renaissance Saint is transformed from a hunter to an animal rights activist. Imagine bankers, leaders of Congress and of Parliament, presidents, prime ministers, and every CEO and each consumer on the planet converting in an instant to the wisdom of nonviolence, as did every great Jain, Christian, Jewish, Islamic, Aboriginal, and all other prophets and sages of any substance.

Morrison offers us each a chance to become St. Eustace, allowing us to embrace the iconic images of paradise that infuse our dreams and the myriad looks of innocence in the eyes of our children and their children. He does so with a vigorous and accessible beauty of language and of a transformative thinking that is akin to *metanoia*, a word best used to describe transformative behavior and intention.

I urge everyone, be they of hope or hopelessness—whether personages cloaked in dashed hopes or those suffused with a desire to be renewed and recover—to read Roy Morrison's latest book. It is a treatise of earnest and telling sobriety, informed by brilliant reasoning and resonant scientific and economic meditation. The very experience of combing through its loving and spot-on multidimensionality, will be a total life-reaffirming act of ecological citizenry. Our democracy demands nothing less than this humbling effort on our part: to join forces with Morrison in working toward the rational solutions he so evocatively sets before us.

Preface

Sustainability Sutra was, as usual, a product of intention and surprise. My books have generally begun with an attempt to answer a question, in this case, the nature of sustainability as a fundamental co-evolutionary force and its implications socially, politically, and economically. I began with the spare sutra form. By its nature, a sutra raises more questions than answers.

The more I worked, the less I knew. Wrestling with the question of how, and if, a market system could respond to the ecological challenge, I wrote the long introduction, attempting, first, to put sustainability in context, and, second, to explore the nature of a global ecological growth strategy as a response quick enough to avert global ecological catastrophe. But my work did not remain within the familiar and comfortable confines of social theory.

To my surprise, my writings on sustainability and ecological civilization led to my work in China. My Chinese counterparts told me that in my book *Ecological Democracy* I had been the first person in the world to discuss in a book an ecological civilization, "the community of communities."

Building an ecological civilization, rooted in Chinese philosophical traditions and practices seeking harmony and balance, had become official Chinese government policy.

My work in China included development with Roger Faulkner and Professor Jennifer Wells on preliminary plans for a China–East Asia Efficient Renewable Electric Supergrid using High Voltage Direct Current (HVDC) transmission to ultimately replace all fossil fuel and nuclear resources with efficient renewables.

I was privileged to present a plenary speech in 2013 on building an ecological civilization to the World Cultural Forum in

Hangzhou that issued the Hangzhou Declaration, a global call for building an ecological civilization in the face of grave environmental challenges. I've subsequently been invited to contribute opinion pieces to Beijing People's Daily, for example, calling for cooperative Chinese and American leadership at the UN Climate Change Conference in Paris in December 2015. I've also helped to edit the English version of Xinhua's annual Environmental Report.

With the encouragement of the publisher Kenzi Sugihara of SelectBooks, I added the twenty-seven sections in *Sustainability Sutra* to clarify and help give concrete examples and resonance to the sutra sections.

Dr. Michael Tobias, ecologist and President of the Dancing Star Foundation, kindly wrote the foreword and encouraged my work.

Sustainability Sutra has benefited from the advice and encouragement I have received from numerous people. Among them I want to thank Pentti Aalto, Roger Ferguson, Robert Timmerman, Dr. Gregor Czisch, Prof. Samuel Miller, Prof. Jennifer Wells, Prof. Herman Greene, Prof. Michael Swack; my partners in building large solar electric systems, George Sahady, Omar Brown, and Steve Hershman of Greater Boston Capital Partners; and my wife, Luanne Baker, and my son, Samuel Schaffer-Morrison. I gained much benefit from the work of Thich Nhat Hanh and from meditation practice. My editor, Nancy Sugihara, is to be commended for both her care and her patience with my work.

What wisdom is to be found in this book, of course, rests upon the work and contributions of many others. The errors are mine alone.

I encourage readers to use *Sustainability Sutra* as a tool for further investigation and for helping catalyze change. I welcome questions and comments.

I can be reached at roy.morrison114@gmail.com.

Introduction

These are challenging, threatening, and opportune times. Climate change and ecological catastrophe is a menace advancing at an uncertain pace with consequences that will touch all of humanity, all of life. Humanity's actions are no longer parochial. They are general and potentially irreversible and tragic.

But our future is not yet decided. What will happen depends, in part, on the concerted actions of all of us. An ecological turn based on the pursuit of sustainability can transform a self-destructive industrialism into a prosperous global civilization, an ecological civilization. The choices are ours to make in the 21st century. The consequences will endure long after us.

Either the rise of an ecological civilization, or a sixth mass extinction, will mark the Anthropocene, the Age of Humanity. These are our epochal choices, no more, and no less. Our history is part of a grand, living, and ceaseless co-evolutionary canvas where we now play a crucial role.

Humanity's self-consciousness and social behavior has become integral to the great co-evolutionary dance of sustainability where life changes the ecosphere as the ecosphere changes life. We must face the significance of this epochal change.

In many ways, this is a what, how, and who book. What is an ecological civilization? How can we make it happen? Who will do it? *Sustainability Sutra* will offer detailed answers to these crucial 21st century questions.

Understanding that both elegance and the devil is found in the details, I offer these introductory capsule summaries to serve as sign posts to where we are going. Brevity, of course, can be a daunting task and challenge. The sage Rabbi Hillel was asked to explain the meaning of Torah while he was standing on one foot.

He replied, "What is hateful to you, do not do to your neighbor. The rest is commentary."

What Is an Ecological Civilization?

A working definition of an ecological civilization is a society (or all societies in the world) in which economic growth results in ecological improvement.

A quantitative definition of an ecological civilization is a society maintaining a balance between the insults of human action on the ecosphere and the regeneration of natural capital.

A formal definition of an ecological civilization is a society maintaining human life in a dynamic and sustainable equilibrium with a flourishing living world, which depends on our ability to make new social choices to change the way we live.

Social justice and fairness is fundamental for an ecological future. An ecological civilization cannot be built in a world with a wealthy high-consuming minority and an impoverished majority. We will sink or swim together.

How Can We Make It Happen?

The pursuit of sustainability is the path toward an ecological civilization. Sustainability represents more than a statement of continuity. Sustainability is a fundamental evolutionary principle and motivating force that we will examine, and that now encompasses conscious human action.

Sustainability Sutra will examine how a global ecological economic growth strategy can lead to both the regeneration of natural capital and the growth of finance capital that are fundamental characteristics of an ecological civilization.

The pursuit of sustainability must be supported by a strong framework of clear economic rules and market price signals. All polluting, depleting, and ecologically damaging goods and services must become more expensive and lose market share. Sustainable goods and services must gain market share and become more profitable. Investment, fiscal, and monetary policy must follow sustainable norms.

Central to the pursuit of sustainability is replacing all fossil fuels and nuclear energy with efficient renewable power. Renewables will not just provide for familiar electric uses. In the 21st century, a renewable electric grid, on a continental scale if needed, will power our cars, heat and cool our homes, and provide energy for processes in our factories. This is a preeminent example of economic growth requiring trillions of new capital investment that will lead to ecological improvement and the regeneration of natural capital along with the creation of millions of jobs.

An industrial ecology based on zero-pollution and zero-waste must be the operational principle and goal for our factories where all outputs become inputs for other processes. Similarly, ecological production principles must govern agriculture, forestry, and aquaculture to stop habitat destruction and ecological damage while using strategies to enhance the process of carbon sequestration and carbon offset to have enormous amounts of carbon act as a means for global cooling.

Who Will Do It?

This is the easiest question to answer, and the hardest to accomplish. All of us are called on to participate in this. It is highly likely that a transformation of this magnitude will require the action of a global mass movement for ecological change to help overcome the power of the polluters and poisoners and their political lackeys. An ecological future will not be handed to us unbidden by Act of Congress or United Nations climate negotiations.

Definitions and brief summaries raise more questions than answers. Is an ecological civilization an emergent quality of a social system? Can an ecological civilization be quantified and a subject for a company's quarterly and annual reports? Is ecological civilization a dynamic process or a stable state? What's a good guide to follow for the practice of this and to help unleash our imagination? Will we seize the moment before ecological catastrophe forecloses our good options?

Moving Ahead

We have the technology; we have the capital and entrepreneurial verve to transform both the global fossil fuel energy systems to renewables and change the polluting industrial infrastructure to sustainable processes; we have the economic and political tools to put high enough prices on pollution, depletion, and ecological damage to help make global economic growth mean ecological improvement; we have mechanisms for ecological and social justice to make a sustainable future the common goal for all of humanity. Exploitation in terms of these goals has come to mean shifting the consequences of pollution, poison, and ecological degradation to the poor. This has given rise to a global movement for ecological justice as key part of global struggles for social justice.

A Transformation to a Global Focus on Renewable Energy Emerges

There are, decidedly, glimmerings of hope for an ecological balance of our planet that we can build upon. We are in the midst of a rapid and accelerating global expansion of efficient uses for renewable energy. This is driven by rapid technological development, plunging costs for wind and solar energy systems, exploding global markets for investment in renewable energy, and active government leadership in response to the clear and present dangers posed by climate change.[1]

Bloomberg Finance's *New Energy Outlook 2015* projects that two-thirds of international energy investment in the next twenty-five years, over 8 trillion dollars, will be made in renewables, in both large scale and distributed renewable energy systems. Much of this will be in Asia-Pacific nations.[2]

China alone will attract $3.3 trillion of new investment—nearly double the total for the Americas, Bloomberg reports. "For every 1 gigawatt of new build in the Americas, 3.4 gigawatts will be installed in [Asia–Pacific]."

Similarly, Deutsche Bank in 2015 is predicting that solar systems will be at cost parity with fossil fuels in up to 80 per cent of the global market within two years. "We believe the trend is clear: grid parity without subsidies is already here, increasing parity will occur, and solar penetration rates are set to ramp worldwide," Vishal Shah notes in his 2015 solar outlook.[3]

Efficiency is also on the march. In 2014, for the first time, the rate of global economic growth exceeded the growth in electricity use. In the United States and Japan, demand for electricity has been flat and is likely to continue to decline. "In the post-financial crisis returning economy, we are using more energy efficiency and doing more with less," according to Bloomberg New Energy Finance lead author Sed Henbest.

A London School of Economics study in 2015 found China's carbon emissions is likely to peak by 2025, at least five years before the 2030 date established for this goal, and this will be followed by progressive reductions. This is very good news. It's crucial to prevent our planet from exceeding a global 2-degree-centigrade temperature increase as a result of climate change.

The United States and Brazil have jointly pledged to raise renewable generation, excluding hydro, to twenty percent by 2030.[4] Hawaii has just announced plans to be 100 percent renewably powered; California plans to be 40 percent renewable by 2030; New York plans to be 80 percent renewably powered by 2050: Vermont's now making utilities responsible for reducing customers total carbon outputs, including heat and transportation.

This is an accelerating global process as solar electric prices continue to plunge. In India, huge factories are being built to make solar electric systems competitive with fossil fuels without subsidies. In the United States a Tesla giga-factory is under construction to build lithium batteries to provide cheap electric storage that can be the basis for a global solar-led energy transformation.

There's much more that must be done and can be done to first stabilize and then reduce global greenhouse gases. This means we must stop burning coal. These decisions must be made. But a global renewable transformation is now in motion.

It's not just machines and mandates. Pope Francis has issued his remarkable, detailed, and pointed June Encyclical document *Laudato Si' (Praise Be to You)* subtitled *On Care for Our Common Home:*

> At one extreme, we find those who doggedly uphold the myth of progress and tell us that ecological problems will solve themselves simply with the application of new technology and without any need for ethical considerations or deep change. At the other extreme are those who view men and women and all their interventions as no more than a threat, jeopardizing the global ecosystem, and consequently the presence of human beings on the planet should be reduced and all forms of intervention prohibited. Viable future scenarios will have to be generated between these extremes, since there is no one path to a solution. This makes a variety of proposals possible, all capable of entering into dialogue with a view to developing comprehensive solutions.
>
> Par 60. *Laudato Si'*

Sustainability Sutra will explore in detail a global ecological agenda as a path toward building an ecologically healthy civilization from industrial business as usual. This means, for starters, investing trillions in building an efficient global renewable energy system to *replace* fossil fuels and nuclear energy that will result in both economic growth and ecological improvement. Similarly, trillions invested in ecological production systems—in sustainable agriculture, forestry, and aquaculture—will support both economic growth and ecological improvement, both the growth of finance capital and the regeneration of natural capital.

A global growth agenda is a recipe to do both good and well. It is not simply a matter of good intentions, of polluters suddenly seeing the light after reading *Laudato Si: On Care for Our Common Home*. Rather, a path toward a sustainable ecological future for our planet will be built as we travel. This is the crucial job for citizens, for government, and for business in the 21st century. We must craft a supporting structure for the future of our ecology, including new market rules, ecological assessments on our consumption, mandates, laws, and regulations for investments in our ecosystem; and durable community-based organizations and structures to support and fight for a prosperous and just future.

Alongside business and government there must be the third strong social force of a world community to establish a process of ecological checks and balances in the 21st century. An ecologically sound civilization will be an expression of the dynamics of our freedom of choice arising from grassroots actions to setting a world community in motion writ large.

A stable and prosperous ecological future will not be handed to us. The poisoners and polluters will concede nothing. They will not simply give up their expected profits from the coal, oil, and natural gas still in the ground or the revenue from their polluting plants. A transformation to an ecological growth system must overcome the power and prerogatives of business as usual intent on wringing the last drop of profits from poison.

The future choices faced by the board of directors of an Exon-Mobile, an Arch Coal, and a National Grid must be either an investment in sustainable prosperity to achieve a rising EPS (Earning Per Share) or following a rough road of declining income, shrinking profits and ultimately bankruptcy and dissolution.

Sustainability Sutra is an ecological investigation to help find our path forward through a dark industrial night toward the dawn of an ecological sun rising.

Sustainability

Sustainability is a fundamental dynamic where life, in response to all influences and circumstances, has evolved and, at the same time, shaped an ecosphere to be favorable for life in all its dazzling manifestations. Evolution has sped up and slowed down in response to changes in the ecosphere. This is sustainability in motion. And now, sustainability, as a fundamental biological dynamic, has become a self-conscious social behavior.

This evolution, occurring as a planet shaping co-evolution, is action on a planetary scale. Sustainability takes advantage of all the instruments in life's evolutionary orchestra including a tendency toward self-organization, exchange of genetic material, symbiosis, cooperation, and complex epigenetic ways and means to control and switch genes on and off. And now, sustainability encompasses social action.

Humanity is now central to the future of all of life, for better, or for worse. Humanity's actions now affect all Earth's species far beyond our own existence as another successful primate.

Sustainability Sutra is a consideration of two paths. First, is the path toward building a prosperous, sustainable future of vital ecosystems. Second is the continuation of a self-destructive business and pollution as usual and an unfolding global sixth mass extinction.

Life has not only created and maintained an oxygen atmosphere with just enough carbon dioxide to maintain a hospitable surface temperature. Life, even in the face of sudden catastrophic change and periodic mass extinctions, has repeatedly been able to survive and once again flourish without privileging any particular species or group.

Sustainability Sutra attempts to help open our eyes to the nature, prospects, and possibilities of the ecological path. It's crucial to understand, as the ice and methane permafrost melts and the climate changes as a consequence of industrial emissions, that the five mass extinctions over the past 500 million years were driven by catastrophic climate-changing geophysical events. Massive volcanic eruptions, or huge meteor impacts, or massive glaciation and a drop in sea levels, changed the climate faster than most species could adapt. Five times in five hundred million years between 50 and 95 per cent of all species living in water or on land perished. Industrial humanity through its effluents can now unleash what was once the province of pure chance, of meteor showers or a change in the dynamics of the earth's core.[5]

In the previous five mass extinctions, while most died, some heretofore marginal species survived and their descendants rose to prominence. *Juramaia sinensis,* for example, the earliest known placental mammal, was our shrew-like ancestor living amidst the dinosaurs 165 million years ago in what is now north east China. It was not until another 100 million years, at the end of the Cretaceous, that a meteor impact led swiftly to the fifth mass extinction with the end of the dinosaurs and the beginning of the Age of Mammals leading eventually to humanity's rise to global prominence.[6]

And now humanity and it's global industrial civilization is rushing like lemmings toward the cliff's edge. But there are paths that lead away from the precipice, toward safety. That's our choice. We can continue rushing toward catastrophe, or take the alternate route.

The Path Toward Sustainability

Sustainability Sutra is informed by the exploration of three basic pillars of sustainability:

First, sustainability as social practice is the resolution of the contradiction between biological and social well-being and change.

Second, the success and the measure for sustainability in the 21st century is for economic growth to mean ecological improvement. Sustainability means, therefore, *both* the well-being and regeneration of natural capital *and* the growth of financial capital as an ecologically productive tool for human betterment.

Third, the global pursuit of peace and social justice is an essential concomitant for the success of a sustainable global growth agenda and building a sustainable future. An ecological civilization cannot be created on a foundation of billions living in poverty and misery, seeking shelter beneath the arrays of solar panels, while a billion members of a global class of consumers lives in comparative renewably-powered luxury.

These three pillars of a sustainable ecological future can be built, strengthened, and maintained through a combination of:

- existing and readily available technology;

- the imposition of new market rules that make the market price system send clear signals for sustainability and guide monetary, fiscal, and investment policy;

- the application of focused government policies to help guide a global ecological economic growth agenda and a global pursuit of justice and fairness supported by durable grassroots social institutions that together lead to a concomitant regeneration of our eco-systems;

- and the nurturance and growth of strong third force community institutions to help balance the power of big business, big government, and big data. This third force arises from grassroots and community power, from cooperatives of all kinds giving people an ownership stake and a voice, from NGOs, from unions, from new institutions of sustainable entitlements, such as a Basic Energy Entitlement (BEE) and a Basic Income Guarantee (BIG) supporting a global convergence on sustainable and just norms and replacing conventional welfare bureaucracies.

We simply cannot resolve the contradictions between biological and social well-being without building durable social, political, and economic structures that support sustainable economic growth, regeneration of natural capital, and ecological justice and fairness for all. An ecological civilization represents a fundamental evolutionary departure from the conduct and consequences of business, pollution, and poverty as usual. This is sustainability in action as both a biological and social force.

I want to be clear. A civilization can be built by carefully crafted policies for reaching sustainable ecological ends from the Right, or Left, or Green perspectives in support of a high profit, ecological global-growth agenda.

What must be on offer is the practice of an ecology platform by the Right, by the Left, and by the Greens. These platforms may differ radically in programs and approaches, but share common goals and objective for a sustainable ecology and a prosperous future.

Globally, we all must have the basis for a decent and ecologically sound life, or it is likely that none of us will. By failing to see the mutual self-interest and the survival imperatives behind both ecological and social justice, we will likely fail to prevent the descent into global ecological catastrophe and a Mad Max future. If the billions of the populations of India, China, Indonesia, and Brazil aspiring to escape from poverty recapitulate a high-pollution industrial pathway, ecological catastrophe is almost certain to follow. The status quo is not an option. The alternative to ecological collapse must be ecological growth and a shared sustainable prosperity for all.

We now have the renewable tools to create a fossil-free and nuclear-free global energy system and, just in time, stop and reverse a seemingly inexorable march toward climate catastrophe. Global warming can yield to a conscious program of an ecological global-cooling agenda driven by removing atmospheric carbon through soil building and reforestation.

An ecological transformation will be manifest with the global implementation of efficient renewable resource development as an industrial ecology, where all outputs become inputs for processes in a zero-waste and zero-pollution economy and by a sustainable agriculture, forestry, and aquaculture.

The path ahead must be global in the pursuit of ecological growth, and ecological healing and justice to reach its goals of a global ecologically successful civilization. But this cannot be accomplished on the basis of simply maximizing the number and the wealth of billionaires and the power of individual nations. The poor cannot be told to wait in line while the rich continue to practice business and production of pollution and profits as usual. The alternative is an inclusive global-growth agenda funded, in part, by investment and technology transfer from rich to poor. This is not the practice of charity, but of productive investment to build the energy and productive infrastructure for our ecological future.

Sustainability Sutra's Point of Departure

Sustainability Sutra's point of departure is from the existing global market economy in a world where billions are poor, where war is endemic, and where pollution and depletion and ecological damage presents a clear and present danger for unfolding ecological catastrophe. This is a world in which achievement of a balanced ecological future will provide for all of humanity a sustainable and prosperous life.

Vandana Shiva, physicist, ecologist, and activist, wrote, "I consciously made a decision to dedicate my life to protect the earth, its ecosystems, and communities. Quantum theory taught me the four principles that have guided my work: everything is interconnected, everything is potential, everything is indeterminate, and there is no excluded middle."[7]

Sustainability Sutra is informed by the belief that it is *possible,* by using the market system to make the requisite changes, to move rapidly toward a sustainable future. This must mean major changes in business and pollution as usual. It means the use of the political, economic, and scientific tools, which are all readily available, to facilitate this transformation.

We do not need a revolution. We do not need to abolish corporate capitalism. We do need to fundamentally change the ecological consequences of business and pollution as usual. But we do need to conduct all economic activity in response to ecological market price signals, market rules and regulations, and our monetary, fiscal, and investment policies that make economic growth. This will lead to a restoration of natural capital, as well as an increase of monetary capital, and will establish the basis for social justice and peace.

We have the technical ability to improve our efficiency by a factor of five or ten, to dramatically decrease total material inputs to practice an industrial ecology leading to zero pollution and zero waste, and to transform agriculture, forestry, and aquaculture into sustainable activities.

With startling alacrity, governments spent tens of trillions to save the global *financial* system from self-destruction in the wake of speculative excess and bail out the speculators and the bankers enabling them.

Our challenge is to apply the requisite social energy and finance to save both the global economic and ecological systems from self-destruction. This is not a bailout, but productive investment in the future of trillions of dollars in capital, creating millions of sustainable jobs and leading to the regeneration of the living world upon which all wealth and health depends.

As a social practice, the path toward sustainability and prosperity must be deliberate. Sustainability must enter the political, economic, technical, and philosophical realms. Once the stakes are understood as being high enough, much is possible. For example, the American automobile industry, at the start of World War II, went from producing millions of commercial passenger cars a year to just dozens a year, while a one-million-part B-24 bomber rolled off the assembly line every *hour*.[8]

What we know now can drive an ecological transformation. What we are learning and its implications remains to be seen once the power of an ecological transformation is unleashed.

What will be the future contribution of an urban agriculture, of vertical organic hydroponics, of urban aquaculture combining fish farming with the recycling of fish waste as fertilizer for greens? What is the role of a carbohydrate economy, of farmers growing plants used for inputs for plastics, fabrics, and chemical inputs instead of petroleum? What will the rapid emergence of nanotechnology mean for energy production at enormously higher efficiency and power density? What are the implications of ever-cheaper photovoltaic paints and building materials, and ever-more-efficient photovoltaic cells combined with low cost battery storage, and with ever more efficient buildings that are inherently net-zero energy consumers?

The time to act is *now*. We cannot wait until irreversible catastrophe is at hand and industrial green house gas pollution has unleashed unstoppable geophysical forces.

Shell Oil, no climate change denier, according to a document from its 2015 "New Lens Scenarios" is planning for the prediction of a catastrophic 4 degree centigrade increase in the short term rising to a 6 degree centigrade increase in global temperature in the long term, far exceeding the 2 degree centigrade average temperature increase established earlier by world leaders as the limit for global warming before we move into truly catastrophic territory. "We also do not see governments taking steps now that are consistent with 2 degrees C scenario," concludes Shell.[9]

The pursuit of sustainability does not require an end to markets or capitalism or economic growth. Sustainability does not mean a world limited to bucolic Vermont villages and small businesses. Sustainability as a transformative and saving social practice simply requires that economic growth must mean ecological improvement and the pursuit of justice and fairness. Sustainability is an expression of an ecological democracy in motion. Sustainability is not limited to the prescriptions and politicians. It can also use the best analysis by the Harvard Business School, cooperatives, and unions and NGOs focused on sustainable ends.

An ecological civilization in China, in the United States, in the European Union, and in an African Union will be different, but will share common practices in pursuit of sustainability and the concomitant growth of natural and finance capital.

Each group will follow their own path, pursue their own initiatives, but in communicative concert with others. We need not, and cannot, wait for global decisions to be made by consensus in United Nations climate talks. We can proceed with unilateral, bilateral and multilateral initiatives *now* in productive, cooperative and communicative pursuit of an ecological future.

Corporate Earnings in the 21st Century

Sustainability must be understood and logically embraced as the saving of business and an ecological solution for all of us. It's easy to say that our worldview must extend beyond the quarterly business reports of earnings per share and be cognizant of seven generations and beyond. What's harder is to make this a dynamic part of everyday reality, where the quarterly earnings report now reflects ecological improvement, such as a decrease in pollution, or a depletion of resources, and ecological damage.

In the 21st century, corporate earnings must be predicated upon and rooted in the improvement and regeneration of the ecosphere, of natural capital, the preservation and growth of monetary capital, and the practice of social justice. Globally, the production and distribution of the social product in the 21st century must reflect, as core self-interest mandated by law and signaled by markets, the creation of surpluses, the nurturance of the living world, and a fair and just distribution to use a portion of the trillions of dollars in profits for the support of ecological justice and elimination of desperate poverty.

If we do not pursue justice, the misery we see on television of the desperate poor afflicted by drought, by flood, and by hunger will likely become an all too accurate vision of a common future. Modest, but systematic, cash transfer mechanisms from rich to poor can dramatically help to alleviate desperate poverty, encourage productive work on sustainability to help provide the material and social basis for improving our ecological future.

The cost of a global program for climate change prevention and mitigation is estimated to be one per cent of global product. In 2013, global GDP was about 74 trillion dollars a year. This means an annual global expenditure of 740 billion dollars a year. This is a lot of money, but reasonable when compared to the trillions lavished annually on the military and throw-away consumer goods, and the incalculable costs and consequences of runaway climate change.

But the notion of considering such investments, as part of a global ecological growth strategy, as a "cost" is wrong-headed. These are transformational investments leading to sustainable economic growth, long-term returns on these investments, and a great expansion of sustainable economic activity. The challenge is how to facilitate and target such investments.

We will examine a Basic Energy Entitlement, a BEE, based on assessments on energy use, as one means to transfer resources from rich to poor to facilitate the transformation of investment in efficient renewable energy technologies to address both climate change and poverty.

Sustainable Ends and Sustainable Profits

An ecological civilization will tend toward dynamic self-management and a great expansion of sustainable trade and sustainable relationships within a context of intelligent limitation. *Sustainability Sutra* focuses on the steps necessary in the context of a global market system to make the changes necessary for the pursuit of sustainable ends and sustainable profits. An ecological market system and an ecological democracy is offered as the path forward instead of calling for the adoption of system X that has no clear vision of getting from here to there and whose first principle is to abolish corporate capitalism.

Sustainability Sutra suggests that we must enter the business and political thicket in the pursuit of sustainability and to follow the path toward an ecological civilization doing whatever must be done to make economic growth mean ecological improvement. We must start not by assuming such a world exists and then function in a manner that addresses a fantasy, but must address the world that is, to find the ways to get from *here,* a self-destructive industrial present, to *there,* a future with an ecology that bodes well for our planet.

Capitalist markets and the pursuit of profit has led to pollution, depletion of resources, and ecological destruction, but that does not mean that communist-planned economies without capitalists have not had similar or worse consequences. Ecological markets require that the pursuit of profit results in ecological improvement for all, by utilizing a production and energy system with a zero pollution, zero emissions production cycle governed by an industrial ecology.

In ecological markets, the system of pricing products must send clear "price signals" for sustainability.

Sustainable goods must become less costly than the polluting alternatives; they must gain market share, and become more profitable. The pursuit of profit will drive an ecological transformation in ecological markets.

This can be accomplished through changes in market rules and regulation, monetary, fiscal, and investment policy, and the use of a comprehensive system of ecological assessments, fees, and taxes to replace income taxation to send clear and strong economic signals throughout global markets and supply chains.

By allowing industry to engage in practices that damage the environment without receiving penalties in what we call "polluting for free" and by allowing cost-shifting of the "externalities" (the code word in the jargon of economics for shifting one of the costs of producing something to others, such as the tax payer, or shifting the responsibility for the hazards or risks of producing the item to other parties not directly involved with the activity), the polluters gain the competitive advantage and put clean competitors out of business. This is our Adam Smith 101. If market economies are to survive and to prosper, it must be through the practice of an industrial ecology with the goal of zero pollution and zero waste. All outputs of production must become inputs for other processes. Nothing is wasted and the costs of production are not passed on to others and hidden. Market prices become the actual total price.

This underlies an ecological economics where the economy is understood to be a subsystem of the ecosystem with an essential goal of the preservation and regeneration of natural capital.

Building a global ecologically sustainable civilization is the prosperous business and entrepreneurial alternative to a dystopian future. It means all polluting businesses must change, and it means establishing the market rules, government policy, and taxation to make good business mean sustainable business. This is not pie in the sky. It is possible, and it is essential.

Automobile companies like Subaru already proclaim that their cars come from landfill-free plants, and GM is committed to landfill-free factories.[10] Walmart's three sustainability goals are to be 100 percent supplied by renewable energy, to create zero waste, and "to sell products that sustain people and the environment." Lennar, the second largest home builder in America, is now including solar panels they own on *all* new houses to provide renewable electricity at a 20 percent discount for homeowners.[11]

Implementing new ecological market rules will make Walmart's, GM's, and Lennar's job much easier. By phasing out "pollution for free," sustainable goods will cost less, gain market share, and become more profitable. Balance sheets in the 21st century and quarterly earnings reports can and must lead the way toward our ecological future.

It is well understood that corporations are, by and large, passing and fungible entities, expressions of their time and their utility. The list of global leaders today will likely be dramatically different in thirty years. And if a global market system is to survive and thrive, the leading corporations in thirty years must be those that responded to the opportunities and imperatives presented by the ecological challenge.

Fiduciary Responsibility in the 21st Century

Fiduciary responsibility in the 21st century must come to mean the improvement of the bottom line, that is, the growth of finance capital, *and* the regeneration of natural capital, *and* the application of measures to systematically reduce poverty and transfer resources from rich to poor.

The 21st century corporate charter must, by law, include the mandate to achieve profits and business goals in a sustainable fashion. Profit, sustainability, and ecological well-being must be made to be fundamentally connected and inseparable. Economic growth and profit can and must be achieved only in the context of sustainable ends and zero pollution-zero waste ecological production cycles whose end result is regeneration of natural capital as a consequences of the growth of finance capital.

The earth can no longer be reduced to consumable and vanishing resources that are turned into cash flows. Monetary and natural capital must exist in a virtuous and renewing circular flow. The action mandated for a sustainable corporation is logically pursued within the context of the new market rules and price signals that encourage and reward conduct aimed to have sustainability.

This ecological path must be global. Global trade rules already allow imports to be required to meet national ecological standards or be subject to paying duties. We must systematically transfer technology to poor nations and invest to help them build their own futures of ultra-low-polluting ecological growth. Thus, creation of a virtuous global-growth circle will be based on prosperity for all. There will be no more wars for oil, for instance, in a renewably powered world. This is a world in which fume-spewing, gasoline-powered cars are anomalies will be exhibited at the country fair as examples of the Age of Pollution.

Recognizing the ecosphere and the commons as natural capital does not mean one more reduction of the earth to benefit business. The awareness of the inseparable nature of the health of the ecosphere and the commons, the growth of natural capital and the growth of finance capital, is a formula for the growth and protection of real and enduring wealth. This awareness of the connection between health of ecosphere and the health of humanity was part of the wisdom of traditional sustainable societies, and it must become part of the wisdom and law for guiding ours.

The accounting methods for keeping track of progress toward an ecological civilization must count sustainable actions as a positive and unsustainable actions as a negative. Polluting activities must be accounted for and understood for what they are—self-destructive destroyers. Countries with markets large and small can limit imports to goods and services that meet the high criteria set that have become our ecological norms in which the most ecologically destructive ones are banned altogether and others are subjected to appropriate and very substantial import duties. The global market will quickly respond to such signals.

Justice and Fairness and an Ecological Future

Sustainable wisdom is, as well, the global expression of justice and fairness, which is essential and inescapable if we are to successfully pursue a stable ecological future. Ecological and social justice in the 21st century needs to be regarded not as an avoidable cost by business, but as an essential pillar for global ecological growth.

Under industrial business as usual, our market systems, unless operating within the context and guidance of intelligent limitation, will result in the following:

◉ The self-destructive creation of externalities, that is, pollution, resource depletion, and ecological damage visited upon those down-wind or down-river, or upon future generations and

◎ Income inequality and the creation of poverty on enormous scales along with the creation of enormous wealth—this is our unsustainable world where an American CEO makes 1,000 times the wage of a comparatively well-paid American worker and 100,000 times that of the poor living on a dollar a day.

This book is not written to be an argument that is anti-market. It unabashedly advances an ecological global growth agenda as an essential, achievable, and available market path toward an improved ecological future.

But, I want to also state clearly: A future built through an ecological global growth strategy is absolutely dependent upon a market that, first, places limitations on ecologically destructive practices and, second, establishes rules that send clear price signals for sustainability and, third, creates a market structure that establishes a global pursuit of social justice and peace as a characteristic of ecological economic growth. And, it is not government alone or markets alone that must be the balancing and countervailing force to business and "pollution as usual." The third force of community social institutions and NGOs must play an important role.

The texture of an ecological market society will tend to be characterized, supported, and protected by a variety of institutions that apply countervailing power to the power of big business and big government. Mechanisms such as a living wage, a negative income tax, a Basic Income Guarantee (BIG), a Basic Energy Entitlement (BEE), provide support both for global ecological justice and an ecological transformation.

Strong unions in support of ecological and social justice are a key for the success and long-term durability of an ecological global growth agenda. Unionization must become recognized as a human right, as suggested by Thomas Geohegan in his book *The Only Thing that Can Safe Us* (New Press, 2015). The aim is an economy rooted in high-skilled, high-wage, and zero pollution jobs where innovation rises from the shop floor in support of an ecological global growth agenda.

An evocative successful model is German co-determination, where workers have half the seats on the boards of largest corporations. The trade-off, in Germany, is a Right-to-Work nation where unions no longer fight for contracts to represent and collect dues from all workers.

From the World Bank to the OECD to the United Nations and to the Potsdam Institute, the basic facts are clear. "Dangerous climate change is a threat to the poor. Intelligent climate protection, on the other hand, can considerably reduce poverty. Global climate protection can only be achieved can only be achieved if a fair offer is submitted to developing and newly industrialized countries that takes their interest into account."[12]

It's important to understand that failure to aid in a global ecological transformation to renewable energy sources will force the poor to utilize the cheapest and dirtiest energy resources. Most renewables, unlike fossil and nuclear fuels, have zero fuel costs and low or zero emissions, but high capital cost. Without access to capital, the poor will not be able to afford renewables, and will turn to what's affordable. And what's affordable will be the dirtiest fossil fuels, particularly in an era where renewables are reducing fossil fuel demand and therefore undermining prices.

A Rising Tide Lifts All Ships

The global phenomena of rising inequality in market economies, as Thomas Piketty made clear in *Capital in the 21st Century*, is definitive refutation for our times of the belief that "a rising tide lifts all ships." That may be true, but too many now no longer have boats, even dinghies, or the opportunity to obtain them.

History includes a cavalcade of visions for a good society, of a Shining City on the Hill, a Great Society, a Square Deal, a Fair Deal, a New Deal. In the 21st century, our aspirations need to be the accomplishment of the task of creating true wealth, healing the planet, and mitigating the trials of the weak and the poor.

We can draw inspiration from our past as we adapt to meet today's challenges arising from the diverse and varied visions of a John Winthrop, an Ann Lee, a Jefferson, a Thoreau, a Walt Whitman, a Fredrick Douglass, an Abe Lincoln, a Sojourner Truth, an Alice Paul, a T.R. Roosevelt, a Eugene Debs, an FDR, LBJ, or an MLK.

Plans for social justice to be considered here, such as a Basic Income Guarantee, have been embraced by such market champions as Milton Friedman and right-wing politicians like Richard Nixon. The historical consequences of market action, of market failure, and of winners and losers must be mitigated through planned government action, through programs and policies that encourage self-management and further work.

Market systems, given the reality of the world, are neither self-healing nor self-correcting in their response both to environmental pollution, depletion, and ecological damage and to poverty created by market failure, discrimination, and the increasing and widening system of structural income disparities.

We must have global ecological economic growth. We must have global social justice and peace. Ecological economic growth is necessary for social justice and peace. Social justice and peace is necessary for global ecological growth.

A Global Convergence on Sustainable Entitlements

A global convergence on sustainable entitlements means that the world cannot support the high-polluting, ecologically destructive rich being enabled by a low-polluting, global poor. We must all find ourselves somewhere in the sustainable middle. Desperate ecological times require global transformative measures.

This means there must be a global convergence of sustainable entitlements for energy, food, and water supported by a global growth agenda and expansion in the trade of information, all within sustainable production and consumption norms. We must shrink our ecological footprints as individuals and as communities and at the same time produce more sustainable wealth.

A global convergence toward sustainable entitlements does not mean the need for the pursuit of any prescribed way of life beyond a common pursuit of the sustainability imperative.

Sustainable entitlements in the 21st century must be more than the monthly receipt of transfer payments through the mail and the monthly payment of payroll taxes. There must be a means to help place a ceiling on ecological damage and a floor on inequality and poverty in order to facilitate building a sustainable ecological future.

An ecological civilization will mean transformation for all of us in the ways we live, with the necessary consequences of much less pollution, depletion, and ecological damage and with the prospect of less work, more leisure, more social connection, more love, more philosophy, more invention. We can consume and trade in dematerialized information in all its forms in a renewably powered cyberspace to our heart's content, but our production and consumption of material items must be governed by sustainable limits.

An industrial civilization operates to maximize output, profit or surpluses, and power with scant attention to pollution, depletion, ecological damage, and it considers natural capital as a consumable and substitutable resource. An efficient ecological civilization, in contrast, operates economically, politically, and socially within sustainable ecological limits. Therefore, by maintaining and improving the health of natural capital, it is possible to decouple the connection between the growth of monetary capital from ecological effect within carefully delineated realms of ecological and economic freedom.

In ecological markets, maintaining and improving the health of natural capital will tend to make material production a steady state exercise where growth is achieved through higher efficiency and the substitution of renewable and common resources for non-renewables. In ecological markets, the highest growth sector will be the trade in information in sustainable renewably powered networks. The ecological impact of n+1 exchanges in renewable energy powered cyberspace is miniscule, and therefore the connection between the growth of monetary capital and the destruction of natural capital has been severed. It is not a coincidence that information is already the highest profit center of the 21st century.

I am a social theorist. I am also working on building solar electric systems using parking lot canopies, roof tops, marginal back lands, and abandoned contaminated "brown fields" in working class cities. The plan is to turn wasted lands into mega-watt scale solar farms producing renewable energy, jobs in the renewable sources industry, and tax revenue while, if needed, decontaminating land. The next step is to network the disparate distributed renewable power sources into both local micro-grids *and* continental scale supergrids to provide all our energy from efficient renewable resources—where the second law of thermodynamics efficiency is improved by a factor of five or ten over the practices of business as usual. This will mean a great increase in the amount of useful energy available. This is a prime example of economic growth leading to ecological improvement.

Sustainability's Global Declaration of Independence

The 21st century requires a new global declaration of independence from business and pollution as usual. We declare our separation from the empire of pollution, resource depletion, and ecological damage. Our liberation will be manifest in our pursuit of a sustainable prosperity for all.

In retrospect, if the pursuit of sustainability is successful, the 21st century will be seen as the dawn of an Ecological Enlightenment, based not on a myth of progress, but on ecological regeneration and sustainable prosperity manifest in the harmony of means and ends.

Sustainability as social practice must be rooted in an effective and ongoing balance between the forces of individual freedom and community, that is, the balance between the one and the many to achieve our goals. The health of one is dependent upon the health of the other. Without individual freedom, a community leads toward autocracy; without community, individual freedom leads toward narcissism and self-destruction.

We must preserve the freedom of the individual and the health of the ecological commons. The freedom of action, and of enterprise, can no longer mean the license to pollute and destroy the foundation of community integrity.

I am suggesting, and people like Wolfgang Sachs and Vandana Shiva may disagree, that the market and the corporation in the context of a full panoply of ecological market rules regulating price signals and laws of monetary, fiscal, and investment policy—and that includes the pursuit of social justice to have a transfer of requisite assets from rich to poor—can and will energetically pursue sustainable growth and ecological improvement.

This is not a one-time fix, but rather an active and ongoing system of ecological balancing and equilibration. The self-interest of polluters and of the rich can no longer be permitted to override the common interest and endanger the health of the global commons.

Sustainability and an ecological democracy require no Hobbesian Leviathan to provide direction and order, nor does it call forth, in the name of freedom, the abolition of the state, as opposed to the democratic limitation of the state, the corporation, and the individual in the interest of the well-being of the commons.

A Twenty-Eighth Ecological Amendment to the Constitution of the United States

We must become either an ecologically focused civilization or remain an industrial civilization. And since an industrial civilization is self-destructive and cannot endure, we have no other real choice for survival and prosperity than to follow a sustainable ecological path.

This means for the United States in our century the passage of a 28th constitutional amendment for ecological rights and responsibilities, codifying for all time the determination to follow a sustainable ecological path. This is not just an Act of Congress that can easily be changed by the next Congress. It will be a basic change to our governing Constitution and will be fundamental law. As such it will be an example for adoption by all other nations and groups of nations and the United Nations. But it is most meaningful if it rises from below, from the determination and demands of citizens, to be adopted by the United States as a beacon for all others.

After the Civil War, the constitution was reshaped by the Thirteenth, Fourteenth, and Fifteenth Amendments for equal protection and due process under the law for all, ending slavery, and guaranteeing all adult men the right to vote. Here is a proposed Twenty-Eighth Amendment on Ecological Conduct.

Amendment Twenty-Eight on Ecological Conduct

Amendment XXVIII

Section 1. The rights and responsibilities to protect, sustain and enjoy ecological well being and health shall be a fundamental principle of these United States.

Section 2. Economic growth in these United States shall be guided by principles under law that leads to the improvement and regeneration of natural capital and the advancement of social and ecological justice.

Section 3. Fiduciary responsibility under law shall be defined as the prudent management of finance capital, the improvement and regeneration of natural capital, and the advancement of social and ecological justice.

Self-Restraint and Ecological Growth

Wolfgang Sachs wrote in *The Development Dictionary:* "Three ideals emerge for conceiving a politics which could shoulder the responsibility of acting for a diverse but coherent world—regeneration, unilateral self-restraint and the dialogue of civilizations. Regeneration takes into account that the royal road of development has vanished since there is no longer any ideal of progress to indicate a common direction. Regeneration calls instead for actualizing the particular image of a good society, which is present in every culture. As for unilateral self-restraint, this can take place of the ideal of interdependent growth. It implies that each country puts its own house in order in such a way that no economic or environmental burden is pushed onto others that would constrain their own path. And, finally, a dialogue of civilizations is imperative as a search for peaceful and sustainable coexistence. . . ."[13]

In the context of an ecological global growth strategy, unilateral self-restraint and the pursuit of a good society, I believe, *can* represent not just limitation, but first-mover competitive advantage. Self-restraint, in terms of an ecological transformation, is based on a massive shift of assets away from polluting, depleting, and ecologically destructive activities into productive sustainable practices and building the infrastructure for a sustainable zero-pollution, zero-waste future.

Self-restraint means, for example, a steady and certain phase out of all emitting fossil fuel technologies and the phase in of efficient networked renewables on both a local and a continental scale. The coal, oil, and natural gas must be left in the ground or under the sea bed instead of being burned with pollutants poured into the atmosphere.

Similar actions need take place throughout all aspects of industry, agriculture, forestry, and aquaculture. The built environment, the productive environment, must become the sustainable environment. Profit seeking and the pursuit of sustainability must become practically synonymous; they must move from a grating oxymoron to common sense.

Self-restraint must be a means of doing both good and well. It requires the ability and political will to resist the self-interested blandishments of polluters fighting to maintain business and pollution as usual, holding on, like grim death, to their continued profits from mega-pollution and its cost shifted externalities.

The material consequences of all activity must meet ecological norms. What is sustainable may mean a world where there is much less stuff produced and consumed, and certainly stuff produced in different ways from different physical materials, and more economic activity becoming information bought and sold in renewably powered cyberspace.

All the regulating and self-regulating tools of a modern economy and technology must be brought swiftly to bear on the necessity to make the pursuit of sustainability and economic growth mean ecological improvement and social justice. As Lincoln said, the nation cannot live half-slave and half free. Neither can the world live half-rich and half-poor.

If the United States or China or the European Union or India, for example, went all-in on the exercise of such self-restraint, they would not only pursue an ecologically sustainable future, but become global market leader in the essential tools for ecological survival and prosperity that must be employed globally. In China, it is already official government policy to build an ecological civilization. The question is not intent, but effective implementation.

But the inertia propelling business as usual buttressed by the political power of polluters defending the status quo is still enormous even in the face of swiftly emergent ecological catastrophe. Globally, UN Climate Conferences have unfortunately, so far, become more the means to protect business and pollution as usual than a venue for the pursuit of sustainability, shared prosperity, global justice, and peace.

This cannot be allowed to continue. Realty and our common future calls for sustainability initiatives, large and small, from the neighborhood to groups of nations, and for a great and insistent nonviolent global rising from below in support of sustainability, survival, justice, and shared prosperity. The self-interested greed of polluters can no longer be permitted in their pursuit of short-term profit, leading us on the path toward ecological catastrophe, mass extinction, the collapse of civilization, and the tragedy of the Anthropocene.

Implementing an ecological global growth strategy *now* should be *job one* for government in partnership with workers and business. We can build through our economic and technological prowess a prosperous, fair, and sustainable global future. That can and must be the future for capital in the 21st century.

There Is No Alternative to Business as Usual?

The nay-sayers and defenders of business and pollution as usual are overwhelmingly in thrall to those who want to continue to profit from pollution as economic and political imperative.

The TINA doctrine (There Is No Alternative) popularized by Margaret Thatcher is expressed both by those with a self-interest in "pollution as usual" and by critics of global capitalism who find that imperatives for profit and for growth make market systems existentially incompatible with a stable ecological future. The progress so far of ecologically inclined social democracies, such as Denmark and Germany, and by innovative states, such as California, suggest that this degree of pessimism is unwarranted. That there are substantial challenges does not mean that there are inherent limits to our prospects for ecological social re-creation.

Two applicable historical analogies that refute the TINA doctrine are the swift disappearance of chattel slavery following the Civil War and the rise of social democracy and environmentalism in the late 19th and 20th century in response to the manifest abuses of workers and the living world by unrestrained and avaricious capitalist industrialism.

An ecological civilization will be understood, in retrospect, as part of the necessary evolutionary path of high-technology market systems. The TINA doctrine combines complacency and self-interested paralysis employed as hollow defenses of business, pollution, and exploitation as usual.

Is Ecologically Sustainable Global Growth an Oxymoron?

Sustainability and a global-economic growth strategy, market driven or not, seems to be a contradiction, and an impossibility to some. Indeed, conferences on de-growth and economic contraction are an increasingly popular exercise for ecological economists. My article advocating an ecological global growth strategy was removed "with extreme prejudice" from the website of the International Association of Ecological Economists, but I say, "Let's put down our preconceptions for a moment. Let's be present. Look at where we are going and where we want to go."

I see that the positive prescriptions offered by apostles of economic contraction like Richard Heidelberg that suggest a renewable transformation are also preeminent exercises in sustainable growth leading to ecological improvement. We are in agreement that continuing the path of doing more of what we are doing is the path to self-destruction. But this must not be the limit to our imagination.

Building an ecologically civilization means the productive investment of many, many trillions of dollars in the energy, transportation, productive infrastructure of a sustainable ecological future. Further, an ecological civilization does not mean a one-to-one substitution of sustainable device for the unsustainable. An ecological civilization means a fivefold or tenfold or more increase in efficiency and the adoption of closed production cycles with zero pollution and zero waste. This is the basis of a sustainable global ecological growth strategy to repair the present for the sake of the future, to do both good and well.

There are more choices for the future of civilization than on or off. Sustainable adaptation is the way of evolution. Are we to remain prisoners of self-serving and self-destructive delusions for the continuation of business as usual until all is lost? We must not be so limited in vision. The sharply ascending and unsustainable biological growth curve can, and often does, turn toward the logistic S shape and flatten out toward the sustainable instead of rising until catastrophic inflection points.

Toward a More Complex and Harmonious Future

An ecological civilization is a re-balancing of knowledge and of application in pursuit of sustainability, the use of civilization's means for a qualitatively different and self-consciously more complex, artful, and harmonious end.

Sustainability is inherently imprecise. It addresses the interpenetration of the ecosphere and civilization, conditioned, as all living creatures are, by the health of the ecosphere. Civilization's actions represent a self-conscious expression of a second nature with powers and destructive consequences that have transcended ordinary biological constraints. Epistemology now redefines ontology.

An ecologically focused civilization applies the full panoply of economic, political, social, and philosophical means for sustainable ends in order to first halt and then reverse the association of economic growth, material, and wealth accumulation with pollution, resource depletion, and ecological destruction.

Sustainability Sutra will consider some of the many specific social, economic, and technical tools that can be applied to help us pursue sustainability and manifest an enduring prosperity. The economist, the engineer, the entrepreneur, the worker, the politician, the philosopher, the poet—all of us have a part and will be called upon to take many roles.

Sustainability Sutra considers not just grand abstract themes of renewal, but how we can build the social and economic superstructure for sustainability. This can mean the application of a disparate variety of complementary elements in building a global renewable energy system and a productive infrastructure of our civilization to develop grassroots social structures in support of an ecological transformation. In 1861 Frederick Douglass wrote as the Civil War was beginning: "We cannot see the end from the beginning. Our profoundest calculations may prove erroneous, our best hopes disappointed, and our worst fears confirmed. And yet we read the face of the sky and may discern the signs of the times. We know the clouds and darkness, and the sounds of distant thunder, mean rain. So, too, we may observe the fleecy drapery of moral sky, and draw conclusions as to what may come upon us. There is a general feeling amongst us, that the control of events has been taken out of our hands, that we have fallen into the mighty current of eternal principles—invisible forces—which are shaping and fashioning events as they wish, using us only as instruments to work their own results in our national destiny."

As Lincoln advised in his first inaugural address, we need to appeal to our "better angels to constructively resolve the disagreements and challenges we face." Failure in our case will mean not just bloody war, but the likelihood of mass extinction and the real risk of global collapse.

Sustainability Sutra is offered as an exploration of sustainability and its aspects. It is meant to provoke thought and to help move us toward constructive action. We have much to gain by the pursuit of sustainability, and too much to lose if we continue on the path toward self-destruction. But the sun is rising.

The Sutra As Oracle and Art

A "sutra" is a Sanskrit word for what was originally a traditional Hindu form of a Vedic "precept" or rule written on palm
leaves. It uses aphorisms and technical terms to impart wisdom
and inspire contemplation. By its nature, it makes use of concise
explanation, instruction, and the poetic. The sutra also gave rise
to many supplemental commentaries.

The sutra became a vehicle for varied Hindu, Buddhist, and
Jainist religious wisdom literature. Sutra entered, over time, the
secular and poetic realm.

Writing a sustainability sutra is an attempt to explore the
implications and complexities of the twofold nature of sustainability encompassing the interaction between the biological and the
social. *Sustainability Sutra* as an ecological investigation occasion-
ally adds commentary to the aphoristic. It is a departure from the
traditional form, but dwells, when it can, within the Sutras concise poetic resonance.

Sustainability Sutra, by holding many mirrors up to reflect the
different aspects of sustainability, attempts not simply to offer conclusions or to instruct, but to capture sometimes surprising glints
and new perspectives that can help catalyze the reader's creative
imaginations and perhaps make the path we need follow in the
future emerge more clearly.

Sustainability Sutra is a meditative journey of self-discovery. It
is a path and record of a writer's and reader's heart-way. It aspires

to discover and realize. It shimmers. It explores, looks, and sometimes finds. It does not chisel eternal truths. It offers philosophical, not religious, claims and does not mean to offend by adopting the name Sutra for its form, and it benefits from and gathers bits of wisdom from what has come before. The errors and weaknesses are mine alone, and for that and for any offense I offer apologies.

The sage Lao Tzu, it's said, did not want to write down and distribute the Tao Te Ching. *Sustainability Sutra* aspires to open doors, not provide settled conclusions.

The Sanskrit root for sutra is *siv,* to sew. This suggests that the original sutras were of pages made from palm leaves stitched together. *Sustainability Sutra* attempts to sew together what have been seen as disparate concepts.

What is known or learned is not simply what is read or what is memorized, but is grasped and felt in a deep confluence of intellect and compassionate feeling, the Hebrew concept of *daat,* conventionally translated as "knowledge," but imparts colors of a deeper meaning, of a profound and ongoing and moral and ethical engagement.

A sutra. Not just a text.

1

Louisiana Before and After

An ecological civilization is not mystery or technological magic, but the fruits of the chosen pursuit of sustainability. This too is civilization.

Civilization is the unexpected fruits of desire manifest, self-consciousness escaping traditional limits and leaping toward new beginnings.

April 2015 was the fifth anniversary of BP's oil disaster in the Gulf in 2010. Five years after the spill, I was standing up to my waist in the ocean in Hollywood, Florida, on the Atlantic side away from the Gulf. A brown pelican skimmed above the clear water that was now flat calm after a thunderstorm has roared past. The water was clear. A large school of minnows was swimming past my legs, closer to the shore then the pelican on patrol. I bent over, held my breath and thrust my face into the water to soak my nose in the healing brine of the great mother ocean whose salt concentration still matches our blood. The ocean from where all life came.

On the one hand, all seems well, with the water clean and life teeming. There's no drilling on the Atlantic Florida coast. And if our idyll is powered by Florida Power and Light fossil fuel and nuclear plants, and the gasoline and diesel for our boats provided by oil companies, that's the price someone must pay where there are oil rigs on the horizon and crude oil in the water.

Of course, it's not that simple, the risks we are courting are planetary, not confined to obvious compromised sacrifices zones and will affect us, all of life with devastating consequences.

The fundamental point of this book is that these consequences cannot only be averted, but through the process of making economic growth mean ecological improvement, we can build step-by-step an enduring, vital, and prosperous ecological civilization. Fail to act for too long will invite collapse and devolution to a Mad Max land future of desperate survivors.

That process and path of making economic growth mean ecological improvement requires a fundamental transformation from reliance upon fossil fuels and nuclear power to the use of efficient renewable energy. This is the path toward enormous economic growth, to ecological improvement, to sustainable jobs, communities, and ecosystems. Energy is a key; it is a necessary step, but by itself, it is not sufficient for an ecological transformation. What can happen with energy can and must happen with industry, with agriculture, with forestry, with fishing and aquaculture, and with all productive activities.

Our concern is how we are doing things right, including in Louisiana with their program for residential solar energy, and how we can do things better to select and implement best practices that will be weaved together to form the fabric of an ecological civilization.

Louisiana 2010

I look back at Louisiana to remember the context that helps shape what is and how this can change. My wife, Luanne, my son, Sam, and I traveled to the Gulf in 2010 to film the consequences of the oil spill. Our original intent in the Gulf was to help clean oil-soaked birds and to film.

I learned quickly this was a romantic dream. The mixture of crude oil and oil dispersant Corexit 9500 was a highly toxic brew readily absorbed through skin and into lungs that sickened thousands and threatened health and life. Just walking onto the oil and the Corexit-soaked beach at Grand Isle in Louisiana for a few seconds made Luanne feel ill. Meanwhile heavy equipment was scraping away the fouled sand for transport elsewhere while other machines filtered, heated, and spayed out the remaining sand. In back channel alleys of Grand Isle I took paradigmatic pictures of large dead fish who had struggled to escape the poisoned water before dying and a dead pelican half buried in the sand.

At hearing after hearing we listened to what amounted to a chorus of lies from the State of Louisiana, from BP, from politicians like US Senator Mary Landrieu, from Ken Feinberg, the disaster paymaster, all singing from a hymnal that found there was no essential conflict between oil and shrimp. The official word from on high became variations on the melody that the long-term destruction and degradation of the Gulf marshes, both as a nursery for life that was the basis for one of the world's great fisheries, and as protector of the Gulf shore from hurricanes, was not caused by a combination of cutting channels and pipelines through the marshes and then poisoning and destroying what remained by the oil.

We interviewed shrimpers, crabbers, fishermen, politicians, climatologists, regulators, attorneys, workers on oil-spill cleanup boats, people living near the beach in Louisiana and Alabama, people who had the misfortune of swimming in the Gulf at the wrong time, doctors, public health workers, activists, and scientists. We learned much from people like Marylee Orr of Louisiana Environmental Action Network (LEAN) and LEAN technical director, Wilma Subra, who have fought an uphill battle against polluters and poisoners and their economic and political sponsors for more than twenty-five years.

And money damages for business losses were sometimes paid for those who managed to make their way through the bureaucratic maze established by BP and administered by Kenneth Feinberg. Feinberg has made a fortune as payments gatekeeper valuing life and death first after 911, then for BP, and after the Boston marathon bombing. If you had the receipts to show business shrunk after the spill compared to last year, that was all right. But the health effects from the oil spill were off limits.

Of course, it's really hard to prove that you were sick because you were poisoned even when blood tests showed presence of high levels of the chemicals in your blood. BP decontamination workers, for instance, were sometimes forbidden to use vapor masks since they would "give the wrong impression." It was up to local physicians like Dr. Robicaux to struggle to keep people alive, and public health activists like Marylee Orr and Wilma Subra to fight the good fight.[14]

When Barack Obama and his family came to the Gulf to show it was safe to swim, the beaches chosen were far from harm's way. The Gulf oil disaster had become an "incident" In the words of EPA administrator Lisa Jackson at a New Orleans hearing on plans for Gulf restoration—a regrettable incident, and not the inevitable consequence of business and pollution as usual.

Louisiana 2015

In 2015, Louisiana had the best in the nation residential tax credit for installing solar energy systems. There's a fifty percent state tax credit and 100 percent tax exemption from real estate tax increases for the value of solar systems. A $20,000 system receives $10,000 state tax credit combined with a 30 percent federal tax credit. A $20,000 PV system costs $4,000. Furthermore, for people without capital, it's possible to use third party leasing programs in Louisiana to install a system at zero cost to the homeowner.

In addition, unlike in other states, there is no limit on total amount of solar and solar savings or caps on so-called net metering in Louisiana, as there is in other states like Maine or New York. Nor is there any detailed interconnection protocols beyond basic safety that make solar installation more difficult.

On the downside, fossil fuel polluting with little economic costs makes electricity relatively cheap in Louisiana, reducing demand for renewables. Further, there is no state Renewable Portfolio standard requiring a percentage of generation to be met by renewables. There is also no program for large-scale photovoltaic installations.

Louisiana, despite enormous wind resources in the Gulf, has resisted offshore wind development while supporting deep-sea oil development in the wake of the great spill. Offshore sources of wind energy offers the possibility of replacing jobs in the oil industry with jobs in large-scale development of wind energy and the marine infrastructure necessary to build and service the specialized ships and barges to support wind-energy systems installation and their servicing.

National Renewable Energy Laboratory (NREL) estimates total offshore wind resources, averaging above 7 miles per hour at 90 meter turbine height, at a phenomenal 294,410 megawatts capacity. *Total* US generation capacity in 2013 was 1,060,000 megawatts.[15]

Louisiana has best practices for residential solar that can be the basis for a national solar transition. We generally don't hear about Louisiana as a national solar energy leader in any fashion. At the same time, Louisiana remains as a stalwart part of the fossil fuel problem.

An ecological civilization will be constructed through the adoption of good practices such as Louisiana's residential solar tax credits. This is not magic or mystery, but open-eyed practice.

Wind and solar—not oil, natural gas, and coal—can power a sustainable Louisiana and employ the workers now engaged in high-pollution activities. Men and women risking their lives on ocean oil rigs can be working on installing wind farms in the ocean and solar farms on land, on roofs and parking lot canopies, and along highways.

Coda 2015

Five years after BP's Deep Water Horizon blowout, medical decontamination regimes had helped many people slowly recover from their exposure to oil and Corexit. Paul Doom of Navarre, Florida, for example, was about to join the Marines just before the spill. Following a swim in the Gulf, with the sheen of oil all around him, Paul became very sick and was confined to a wheelchair with a variety of muscular and neurological symptoms. He is now walking and has a family.

Five years later, BP commercials filled the airways extolling their new-found commitment to safety and their claims of the recovery of the Gulf. Meanwhile drilling and blow out accidents continue in the Gulf, such as the April 1, 2015 PEMEX rig explosion and fire, initially killing four and injuring forty-five.

And in July 2015, BP and the Gulf States reached what was billed as an epochal settlement for $18.7 billion for the Deep Water Horizon oil spill, the largest such settlement in US history.

The settlement was received warmly by investors. Pay-off will be made over a decade's time, and therefore not force BP to sell oil and natural gas assets to pay up. At the same time, new huge oil and natural gas projects are likely to come on line with a flood of new cash. BP's future now looked bright and had moved from a "hold" to a "buy."

In addition, of the $18.7 billion, $13.2 billion is not categorized as a penalty in the proposed settlement to be submitted to the federal court, and therefore probably will be considered tax deductible. U.S. Public Interest Research Group (US PIRG) says this would mean the whole deal would be worth only $14.08 billion to the public.

Federal Judge Carl Barbier had found BP "grossly negligent" for the Deepwater Horizon disaster. Penalties alone could have reached $18 billion for violations of the Clean Water Act. Transocean, the drilling rig owner and operator, was also found negligent as well as Halliburton, but it was BP that was ruled 67 percent responsible.[16]

In 2015 the fossil fuel future once again looked bright for BP. True, the global price for oil has plunged and shows no signs of recovering as global investment in solar energy soars, and electric vehicles roll off assembly lines at an increasing pace, while the talk on Wall Street is about trillions in PV investment and a new energy paradigm.[17]

But meanwhile, they were toasting their good fortune in the boardroom of BP, and back to their old business model: get concessions to drill as economically as we can, wherever we can, and sell the product for as much as we can through long-term and spot contracts. In Louisiana, former Governor Bobby Jindal campaigned again for the Republican nomination for president after taking credit for the BP settlement that helped fill the coffers in Baton Rouge and enabled him to fight off both any new taxes and any spending increases regardless of the great needs in a state with many, many problems. Senator Mary Landrieu, despite her valiant efforts in the cause of oil and shrimp, lost her bid for reelection to an even more loyal Republican challenger.

In the world of BP commercials and in the minds of some Louisiana politicians, happy days were here again. There is, and has never been, any conflict between oil and shrimp, and no connection between oil and shrinking marshes, rising seas, and intensifying hurricanes. How can there be?

Sun Rising Sutra

Life is poetry.

◻

Civilization is prose, conditioned not just by understanding, but by application, by agriculture and the rise of the machine.

◻

Civilization is an animal becoming suddenly self-conscious as world-shaper, master of empire, and the mega-machine.

◻

Civilization meant writing, math, metal tools, food surpluses and also the mega-machine of imperial hierarchies, the imposition of slavery and organized violence as war in the interest of empire.

◻

Civilization is the unexpected fruits of desire manifest, self-consciousness escaping traditional limits and leaping toward new beginnings.

◻

An ecological civilization is a departure from the expected course of 21st century commercial empire, a new path of re-creation and re-discovery.

◻

An ecological civilization is a new flower in life's garden, the practice of re-enchantment, and therefore a return. Poetry's return.

An ecological civilization is the collective opening of eyes and minds to the promise and power of sustainability.

An ecological civilization is a rebalancing of knowledge and of application in pursuit of sustainability, the use of civilization's means for a qualitatively different and self-consciously more complex, artful, and harmonious end.

An ecological civilization aspires to economic growth as means for ecological improvement.

An ecological civilization applies the full panoply of economic, political, social and philosophical means for sustainable ends in order to first halt and then reverse the association of economic growth, material and wealth creation with pollution, depletion and ecological destruction.

An ecological civilization employs these social, political and economic means to release the Gordian knot binding civilization to ecological self-destruction. This is not a mystery or technological magic, but the fruits of the chosen pursuit of sustainability. This too is civilization.

An ecological civilization is therefore an expression of the balance of freedom and community that supports and determines the technology of the ecological path.

◘

An ecological civilization is not just the civilization of engineers following principles of an industrial ecology of zero pollution, zero waste where the end products of any process become inputs for another. An ecological civilization is also the civilization of philosophers and poets, the ideals of a Pericles, a Jefferson, a Thoreau, a Whitman manifest in our times.

◘

Freedom and community's ecological path has technological manifestations, but this is wrapped in and codetermined by the dramatically varying political, economic, social, and philosophical structures shaping an ecological turn. ◘

Freedom without community is given to self-destructive excess. Community without freedom is given to tyranny and the rise of the mega-machine.

◘

Community, for an ecological civilization becomes coextensive and consonant with life's community.

◘

Freedom for an ecological civilization is the practice of sustainability and the restoration, repair, and health of the earth and ecosphere.

Natural capital is more than just an oxymoronic attempt to monetize nature and to quantify so-called ecosystem services. Natural capital is, in fact, the basis for the creation, maintenance, and growth of all capital. Without its sustainable basis, monetary capital would swiftly vanish as a consequence of the self-destructive path of business and pollution as usual.

On the block labeled poetry, another face is labeled self-interest, another sustainability, another profit, another freedom, another community, another life.

2

Climate Change and U.S. Politics

*Sustainability is the Ur path of evolution giving
the one and the many the power to shape and co-evolve
with the earth and its ecosphere.*

Sustainability is life's social practice of return to balance.

Shouting Without Listening

Political discourse in the United States has become a conversation of passion without self-examination, mutual understanding, or compromise. This is more than a case of tunnel vision of the Right and Left, or a consequence of the rise of finance capital and the corruption of politics by big money.

This is occurring at a time when fundamental ecological problems threaten either self-destruction or offer the opportunity for fundamental healing and prosperous change. On the surface, we're witnessing another periodic eruption of the paranoid impulse in American politics, the Know Nothings in modern dress, or corruption redolent of a new Gilded Age, but this time with a new and potentially self-destructive ecological twist.

The Right advances positions of market absolutism, beliefs that unrestrained market forces are the self-correcting solution to all problems, and that the use of private property includes the freedom to pollute, deplete, and destroy ecosystems. The Left advances positions that economic growth and markets are irredeemably connected to ecological self-destruction, and that the only solution, without regard to actual consequences of economic

49

activity, is economic contraction and a deliberate policy of de-growth. In social terms, the motto on the Great Seal of the United States, *e Pluribus Unum*, meaning "Out of many, one," is largely ignored in the 21st century.

The current painful political machinations are a reflection not just of the loss of civility, but of deep dysfunction in the fundamental role that the balance of freedom and community must play in building and maintaining a vital democracy and building a viable ecological future. What's most striking is that freedom and community (or justice) are now used as ideological clubs wielded by Right and Left to pummel their opponents. Barack Obama is called Hitler for adopting Mitt Romney's plan for requiring purchase of private health insurance; Obama's opponents are similarly called fascists. A group of largely center-right politicians are now condemned as 1930s fascists by their opponents. Barack Obama and his Republican opponents are many things, but one thing he and they are certainly are not are fascist proponents of National Socialism.

A website, Now the End Begins, in 2015 offers 13 similarities between Obama and Hitler.

> The similarities are terrifying, the conclusion inevitable. On March 23, 1933, the German Parliment (sic) met to consider passing a bill that Adolf Hitler had created called the Enabling Act. It was officially called the 'Law for Removing the Distress of the People and the Reich.'. . . The only fly in the ointment was that the Nazis had, behind the scenes, caused the distress themselves by creating the crisis, so that they could step in and solve it. Sound familiar?[18]

On the Left, a website *Ascending Star Seed* offers:

> My conservative friends and readers. . . . Why is you (sic) are blind to the fact that these Tea Party and Republican candidates are the proverbial wolf in lambs clothing? . . . Can you not see they are fascists, plain and simple. Before you answer

that, if you don't know what fascism is look it up—Hitler and
Mussolini were fascists . . . please study political science for a
refresher because fascism is the road where the Repulicons and
Teabaggers are taking us.[19]

These are the kind of rhetorical extremes practiced before the
Civil War between secessionist slavers and union abolitionists,
between proponents of racist chattel slavery to support feudal style
plantation agriculture for the mass production of cotton and the
free-labor industrial capitalism of the north that drove the country to a civil war. While the passions seem similar, and the question of a Black man in the White House certainly plays a part
in the current shouting match, the issues that appear to tear the
country apart, such as the precise nature of health care policy, the
management of entitlements and the budget, the degree of financial regulations, the nature of a treaty with Iran to limit nuclear
development, are more a difference in quality then in kind.

The Republican party, historically the leader in conservation
and environmental protection from T.R. Roosevelt to Richard
Nixon, and a tradition continuing through the regime of George
H.W. Bush, has strangely and uncharacteristically become the
party of climate change deniers and of environment polluters.
How the party of the owners and supporters of capital are willing
to put all at risk in support of the short-term profits of fossil fuel
polluters is inexplicable.

The British conservatives, in contrast, are in power advancing
their version of a conservative Green agenda to control climate
change. The British right wing have developed comprehensive
plans in accord with the mandates of the British Climate Change
Law of 2008.

It would be very useful for American conservatives to read
the British Climate Change Act and then examine the business-
friendly policies adopted by the conservative government. The
current program combines plans for large-scale offshore wind

development and European Supergrid development to move renewable power between nations, including links to Iceland, with plans for large-scale nuclear development involving enormous government subsidies through guaranteed high-power prices to be paid by energy consumers and using natural gas fracking to replace coal. The nuclear plans are facing major problems from just-discovered design flaws in the new French reactor design that was to be the lynchpin of a new wave of reactors. In addition, the subsidy program may run afoul of European commission rules against these kind of market-distorting subsidies. The British conservative government climate change polices, I believe have major flaws, but they represent a serious effort to have an 80 percent reduction in greenhouse gases by 2050 from 1990 levels:

The British Climate Change Act includes:

2050 Target. The Act commits the UK to reducing emissions by at least 80 percent in 2050 from 1990 levels by Building a Low-carbon Economy.

Carbon Budgets. The Act requires the Government to set legally binding 'carbon budgets.' A carbon budget is a cap on greenhouse gases emitted in the UK over a five-year period. The first four carbon budgets through 2027 have been legislated.

The Committee on Climate Change. To advise the Government on emissions targets, and report to Parliament on progress made in reducing greenhouse gas emissions.

A National Adaptation Plan. Requires the Government to assess the UK's risks from climate change, prepare a strategy to address them, and encourage critical organizations to do the same.[20]

The Republican Party has essentially become a minority party based on the national popular vote. But the Republican Party has achieved much success in Congress and in red states by using clever gerrymandering and appealing to base voters to control Congress. The party has taken advantage of wealthy sponsors particularly in the wake of Citizens United decision, and relying on its appeal to angry white men and evangelicals offering an anti-immigrant, anti-environment policies, combined with anti-gay and anti-abortion politics. At the same time, it has deeply alienated broad swaths of voters.

I believe it is now impossible for the Republican Party to elect a climate-denier president and that 2015 represents the high water mark for Republican climate change denial, much like the high water mark of Confederate advance toward Cemetery Ridge during Pickett's change at Gettysburg before it was repulsed.

A global growth strategy for prosperity and ecological survival can be a political wining program for a 21st century Republican party whose roots are steeped in embracing the connection between economic growth and ecological health. For Republicans to fail to take steps in this direction, is to find themselves as a 21st century version of the Know-Nothing Party.

In 2015 a Yale study finds that solid majorities of moderate and liberal Republicans, 30 percent of the party, think global warming is happening. It's time for the majority of Republicans to return to their roots as the Wide Awakes leading up to the Civil War, but this time awakening the nation to the threat of climate disruption.

It is likely to be a future Republican president who, like Lincoln, seizes the political opportunity, speaks the truth, and leads the nation in solving the existential threat poses by climate change. An emerging solar green tea alliance is signs of things to come.

A Green-Tea Solar Alliance

To what extent solar progress can happen nationally in the United States is an open question given the resolute opposition of their fossil fuel industry and their still almost wholly owned subsidiary, the national and state Republican parties is unclear.

Indeed, there is an anti-solar push back in some states such as Arizona by fossil fuel utilities threatened by solar energy attempting essentially to charge customers for installing PV. It is also interesting that a countervailing force is emerging from right wing and tea party circles embracing solar power for its ability to provide people with self-sufficient and non-polluting energy.

In Arizona, Barry Goldwater Jr. strongly opposed the Arizona Power and Light's attempt to charge customers $100 a month for installing PV solar power that he passionately advocates. Now, the public power utility Salt River Project has jumped on the anti-solar bandwagon.

"Utilities are working off of a business plan that's 100 years old, kind of like the typewriter and the bookstore." On his website, Goldwater says, "Republicans want the freedom to make the best choice." Conservatives are the original environmentalists, he told the *New York Times*, [People] "came out here and fell in love with the land." His father Barry Goldwater Sr. told him, "There's more decency in one pine tree than you'll find in most people.[21]

Senator Angus King from Maine introduced a bill called The Free Market Energy Act of 2015 to guarantee people's right to generate renewable power and to limit utility charges to $10 a month.

> Whether it's solar panels on the roof or battery storage in the basement, advanced technologies are unlocking America's energy future by literally bringing power to the people. But policies governing how these technologies connect to and interact with our nation's electricity grid are stuck in the past and, as a result, are holding back the enormous potential for these technologies to flourish," Senator King said. "My legislation would create a set of guidelines with deference to the states to protect the right of people to connect their technology to the grid, ensure that grid-owners and operators receive their due compensation, and support the continued development of energy resources that will define our future. I look

forward to working with my colleagues, industry stakehold-
ers, and utility companies as we move forward on this important issue.[22]

It's interesting to note that the use of Solar City's battery system that eliminates the "demand" charges imposed by a utility
company on customers who use energy at hours of peak demand
could unintentionally be the basis of a "utility-death spiral" when
customers with storage and renewable generation have increasingly less need for utility power. If the utility clings grimly to
their old model, rapidly emerging solar technologies means they
will die. But we don't have time to allow such dynamics to play
out; we need to make utility rules and structures encourage a
prosperous and sustainable future for all.[23]

In Georgia a Green Tea Coalition alliance has been organized
to fight for solar in red states. A growing split in conservative
ranks between supporters of pollution and business as usual and a
prosperous renewable future is a sign of things to come.[24]

The Breath of Life Sutra

Sustainability is the collective breath of life breathing in and breathing out.

Sustainability is life's meta-communication with the earth.

Sustainability is the Ur path of evolution giving the one and the many the power to shape and co-evolve with the Earth and its ecosphere.

Sustainability's wonder inclines to the fractal, a mirror image of life's dynamic all scales within nested ecosystems from the microscopic to the planetary.

Life's self-organization, reproducibility, and creativity are expressed by individual organisms, but extends far beyond the organism.

Sustainability's elements are the response to all influences; the sending of signals, feedback, and response; self-organization; cooperative action; chaotic dynamics that together serve to maintain an ecosphere and Earth optimally suitable for life, all life, without privileging any particular species.

Sustainability is thus an evolutionary, cybernetic process of life acting globally as co-evolutionary force within the ecosphere for the health of all life.

◻

Sustainability in motion is an expression of chaotic dynamics in service to homeostasis, chaos employed to reduce entropy. Sustainability is life's creative, emergent legerdemain.

◻

Sustainability is life's social practice of return to balance.

◻

Sustainability thus represents both a challenge and an affront to the suzerainty of the mega-machine.

3

Freedom and Community
in the 21st Century

James Lovelock's naming of Gaea is more than a scientist's metaphor. It a description of the Earth's planetary life system. Sustainability is the pulsing polyrhythms of Gaea.[25]

An ecological civilization can and must be built through a creative interaction of freedom and community. Community is not reduced to the tyrannical imposition of the state. Community is soil for the growth and flourishing of freedom. Freedom is the product of community and the protector of the community from tyranny. Freedom is an expression of Isiah Berlin's balance of freedom to, and freedom from. My right to swing my fist ends where your nose begins.

The rise of fascism and communism in the 20th century, in response to the crises, abuses, war, and depression of industrial capitalism, provided object lessons of the horrendous abuse of Nazism and Soviet totalitarianism and of the practices of the state in the name of the community, crushing all freedom.

But if the practice of freedom in the 21st century means the freedom to destroy the global ecological commons, then freedom, along with community will perish. An ecological civilization must be built on strong foundations to maintain in dynamic balance both freedom and community. This balance will be forever contested terrain to be mediated by democracy resting upon guarantees and practice of universal human rights.

This is democracy not limited to a quadrennial plebiscite for president, but democracy structured by principles of subsidiarity providing the most authority to those most directly affected. Thus a national or international mandate to reduce green house gases 50 percent by 2050 from 1990 levels means local choices by a town meeting on how a town implements a local plan, with a local producer making technological choices to reduce emissions by taking advantage of a variety of sustainable investment incentives.

Let's turn down the political noise, and take a step back, and view freedom and community, the relationship between the one and the many, in more basic terms. In doing so, we will quickly come to understand that we can no more separate the one from the many then we can separate the tree and the forest. It is neither a market fundamentalism rooted in individual action, nor the imposition of state power in the name of community that can lead us toward a sustainable future.

A prosperous and sustainable ecological future is dependent upon our ability to pursue freedom and community, expressed as economic growth and ecological health. Our challenge is to embrace *both* freedom *and* community and to hang together and make common cause, as Franklin cautioned, at the signing of the Declaration of Independence, "or assuredly we shall all hang separately."

Even anarchism, in practice, is usually about self-management, the exercise of freedom and community within the context of voluntary participation without the need for the imposition of rules by the state.

Freedom and community are not fundamentally in conflict. Their extremes are in conflict. Freedom and community are best understood as interdependent qualities. Without community, freedom is self-destructive narcissism. Without freedom, community becomes crushing and self-destructive totalitarianism.

Sustainability and Gaea Sutra

Sustainability writ large is the earth as Gaea, a living system manifesting the attributes of life as collective, dynamic, communicative, responsive, and evolving entity, the ecosystem of ecosystems.

⊡

Gaea does not inhabit the earth as a kind of super-organism. Gaea is an integral, living expression of the ecosphere that it shapes and, at the same time, is shaped by and co-evolves with the ecosphere. The figure and ground, subject and object perform an endless creative dance. Gaea is a manifestation of sustainability.

⊡

This twofold nature as actor and acted upon is crucial for understanding living systems and life's mechanisms including sustainability as one as Gaea's basic habits and tools.

⊡

James Lovelock's naming of Gaea is more than a scientist's metaphor. It is a description of the earth's planetary life system. Sustainability is the pulsing polyrhythms of Gaea.

⊡

Sustainability's ambit encompasses all influences and actors, including self-conscious humanity.

4

Failures of
Market Fundamentalism
and Climate Change

Sustainability is the essence of the present in response to all influence and circumstance, and yet it is the shaper and conditioner of the future.

While market fundamentalists, like Hayek, have found markets always far more adept then the imposition of plans by states, the global financial collapse of 2008 made clear the self-destructive power of unlimited economic freedom as a result of the unregulated speculation in complex trades of derivatives in credit default swaps.

Self-serving economic freedom leading to bankruptcy and either collapse or massive government bailouts is hardly what would be desired or chosen by market fundamentalists. Community-imposed limits are clearly necessary to prevent the destructive consequences of black swan events. There are limits to what can be accomplished simply by the exercise of free minds in free markets.

There are several basic reasons for the failure of the ability of free market policies to solve most economic and social problems, (the strong belief known as market fundamentalism that markets by themselves will lead to both optimal and just economic and social ends). There are, in fact, inherent weaknesses in real world market systems on a basic level and that are also a reflection of the general incapacities of freedom without the balancing and self-healing limits of community.

Four Crucial Weaknesses of Market Fundamentalism

1. *Lack of knowledge by market participants, particularly of complex financial instruments*

The invisible hand of Adam Smith can work well when a large number of market participants, both buyers and sellers, share accurate knowledge. The conditions of an agricultural crop can be well understood by observers. And the risk from weather, insects, disease, and even unforeseen events for both farmer and food processor customers can be mitigated through the use of hedge contracts as a beneficial risk-reduction financial mechanism. Classic commodity hedges guarantee both farmers fair and predictable income and the processors fair and predictable prices, but the same is not true when it comes to complex financial derivatives.

As sage an investor as Warren Buffet found the complexity of the new derivative instruments so opaque, in terms of accurately understanding risk, that he termed them financial instruments of mass destruction. The decision to allow banks to self-regulate derivative risk meant that in exchange for booking large profits from peddling derivatives, they risked nearly instant insolvency when the housing market collapsed and the trillions of uncovered speculative bets turned against them.

Interest rate swaps and credit default swaps would lead to either financial collapse and dissolution or sale of some of the largest investment banks or, in most cases, the enlistment of taxpayers as lenders of last resort, in exchange for neither preferred stock interest in future profits (Warren Buffet's offer to Lehman Brothers), nor government stock ownership, board control, and new management as was required in exchange for the GM bailout. Trillions were paid out. The bankers kept their fortunes and their jobs; none went to jail while millions of people lost their homes and millions of workers lost their jobs in this exercise in lemon capitalism where government socialized the losses of the rich and the poor paid the price,

After Canadian banks had escaped the financial collapse of 2008, when interested in investing, I read the annual report of Bank of Canada and found many, many footnotes describing ultra complex and essentially incomprehensible derivative trades involving the banks. They apparently escaped the fate of many others by a prudent combination of less leverage and the oversight of regulators. Canadian banks maintained much higher asset coverage ratios.

At the time of the financial collapse many US banks owned capital assets of equal to only three percent of their total liabilities. That meant that they were leveraged thirty-three to one. For every hundred dollars the bank had at risk, it was only backed by three dollars in capital. If a mere five percent of bad loans and, in particular, financial instruments like the credit-default swap failed, the banks would quickly become financially insolvent. They had made huge profits by underwriting, for a fee, trillions of speculative credit default swaps. The global financial system was quickly pushed into panic once counterparties demanded payments for these swaps they'd bought once mortgage backed securities that these swaps were written against started to fall.

2. *Externalities and the failure to send accurate price signals*

Market systems are based on getting the prices right. By shifting the costs of pollution, depletion, and ecological damage to others and to future generations a market system cannot provide either optimal or just and sustainable consequences. Getting prices right for ecological goals through new market rules is a key to the future existence of the market system and obviously transcends market fundamentalism.

The failure of market systems to properly account for externalities, and the willingness to discount the value of a sustainable future are, of course, crucial leaks in the boat that must be fixed to allow a market system to continue to function and avoid self-destruction and to convert profit seeking into an ecologically sound activity.

Such leaks in the boat are perhaps better understood not as "externalities," but rather as failure in the essential balance between freedom and community whose maintenance is central for the ongoing success of an ecologically sound civilization. Such a system is continually challenged and must be continually readjusted. An effective ecological balance in a civilization is not a static or timeless process. Amendments and adjustments must be ongoing and continuous.

3. *Failure to connect the essential need for an increase in money capital and the health and regeneration of natural capital*

For economic growth to mean ecological improvement, the price system must send clear signals for sustainability by getting the prices right, by redefining fiduciary responsibility and corporate profit seeking to combine and redefine profit as a growth of **both** finance **and** natural capital.

This means the health of markets and the heath of natural capital are inseparably connected. The destruction of natural capital will mean the destruction of monetary capital. The health of finance capital and the health of natural capital must be understood to go hand in hand. By making the price system send accurate signals for pollution, resource depletion, and ecological damage makes it much easier to integrate the finance and natural capital through the operation of robust market mechanisms. To oppose market fundamentalism does not mean opposition to markets.

4. *Failure to account for discrimination and bigotry*

Discrimination can be expressed through institutional practices such as red-lining, denial of education and public services, establishing quotas and exclusion based on race, sex, gender, sexual preference, nationality, housing and community exclusions, and the allowance of the creation of slums and ghettos. This cannot be accounted for, or cured by market fundamentalism.

It is the equilibration of both freedom and community that is the path toward building a successful ecological future to avoid the storms of market tempests and the shoals of government power.

Sustainability Is Life's Way Sutra[26]

Sustainability is life's process and means within ecosystems of all sizes and extents. Sustainability is life's way.

⊡

Sustainability is life's collective, adaptive survival response.

⊡

Sustainability is the essence of the present in response to all influence and circumstance, and yet it is the shaper and conditioner of the future.

⊡

Sustainability is both the heart of the now, and the sculpture of the then. Sustainability is, as well, the record of the before, of life's history and co-evolution with the ecosphere.

⊡

Sustainability thus sees the world with open eyes, and, at the same time, faces ahead and behind.

⊡

Sustainability is a collective attribute of life co-evolving with its ecosphere.

⊡

Sustainability is means and end that has enabled life to survive periodic mass extinctions and once again thrive.

Sustainability is thus implicated both in the creation of our human-driven, sixth mass extinction through industrial pollution and in the healing and counter-vailing social response.

Sustainability has been world shaper, the chemist responsible for the finely balanced oxygen, nitrogen, and carbon atmosphere without self-consciousness to produce and maintain an ecosphere most suitable for life. Life breathes in carbon dioxide and breathes out oxygen; life breathes in oxygen and breathes out carbon dioxide. Sustainability is the co-evolutionary force and process that practices a wonderful parsimonious economy of action to craft enduring balances between plant and animal, predator and prey for the benefit of all.

Sustainability is history's and evolution's greatest gift, the ability of life to reshape itself and the earth in response even to the most catastrophic and sudden changes.

Evolution has meant not just random variation and survival. Evolution is rooted in sustainability and its complex pathways leading to the coevolution of life and ecosphere, reshaping the nature of both.

Human self-consciousness with sustainability becomes social practice, and social movement is a part of sustainability's surprising trajectory and protean power.

◻

What was sustainability called before it had a name and a face? Life's dance?

◻

Sustainability could not have existed as a concept when biology was rooted in a sense of eternal *isness* before an understanding of evolution. The world was seen and felt as timeless fodder to be input for the sake of human progress, to be consumed, disenchanted.

◻

Sustainability existed before there was language.

5

The Ecological Model, and a Circular Economy

Symbiosis is a fundamental aspect of sustainability. The cooperative integration of the web of life is basic, not secondary.

Instead of embracing a market fundamentalism that chooses freedom at the expense of community or embracing a new all encompassing technocratic world that supports community at the expense of freedom, we will be well served by understanding the crucial role that must be played by the interdependence of freedom and community and its applications.

Ecosystems from the pond to the planet are paradigmatic expressions of freedom and community in motion governed by complex cybernetic feedback loops. Sustainable ecosystems are characterized more by the logistic, S-shaped curve, where population growth flattens out to sustainable limits, and not the log curve of accelerating growth chasing the heavens, leading to sudden collapse.

In ecological terms, freedom and community in action forms the structure of sustainable limits and the ability of life to respond to all influences and to make changes that create and maintain conditions most favorable for all life, certainly not for just one individual or one species.

This is the process of co-evolution between species changing as circumstances change as the ecosphere is similarly influenced by the change in species. The world changes, and we change, and the world again changes in the endless cycle of sustainability, a process of the interdependence of the one and the many, of freedom and community.

Building an ecological civilization will mean the pursuit of a global ecological growth strategy in which economic growth leads to ecological improvement. This means the practice of economic growth within the context of sustainable price signals where sustainable goods and services become less costly, gain market share, and become more profitable. Unsustainable goods then become more costly, loose market share, and become less profitable.

The structure that supports such economic and ecological success is an artful and dynamic structure of freedom and community. This will require the practice of a production ecology in all aspects of economic activity where all outputs become inputs for future production processes aspiring to zero pollution and zero waste.

This is the pursuit of economic growth that is designed to enrich not just the present, but the seventh generation. It makes the growth of money capital synonymous with the preservation and regeneration of natural capital.

In classic economic terms, it means an end to externalities, because the market price includes all costs related to the production cycle and costs are not shifted to those downwind or to future generations.

A Circular Economy

A 21st century industrial ecology means the practice on a general scale of a circular economy. Even the capitalist elite has made the consideration of steps to encourage an evolution to a circular economy of material reuse and recycling the theme of the 2014 World Economic forum Davos gathering:

> Today's "take-make-dispose" economy has long relied on inputs of cheap and available resources to create conditions for growth and stability. . . . In its most extreme manifestation,

the global economy is a massive conveyer belt of material and energy from resource-rich countries to the manufacturing powerhouse China, and then on to destination markets in Europe and America where materials are deposited or— to a limited degree—recycled. This is the opposite of a loop. The materials leakage points and barriers to mainstreaming the new model of circular material flows in a globalized economy must now be addressed and overcome. This requires better understanding of the archetypes into which supply chains fall, and the three main barriers to change: geographic dispersion, materials complexity, and linear lock-in. Analyzing the most advanced business cases confirms that a supply chain management approach that balances the forward and reverse loops and ensures uniform materials quality is critical to maximizing resource productivity globally. The transition can begin once the hinge points are identified and acted upon in a concerted effort—across companies, geographies, and along the supply chain.

(Ellen MacArthur Foundation and McKinsey & Company, 2014).

The technical, economic, and political tools are available for the construction of an industrial and production ecology encompassing all aspects of human activity. The pursuit of sustainability will be to create a circular, zero-pollution and zero-waste system where all outputs of one process become useful inputs to another, to improve efficiency of processes by an order of magnitude, and have the price system and regulatory system send clear signals for sustainability for all goods and services. This represents a complete and saving transformation of business and markets as usual whose nature extends far beyond the Davos agenda.

Examining textbooks for industrial ecology (Graedel and Braden R. Allenby, 2010), plans for continental scale renewable energy grids (Faulkner, Morrison, Wells, 2013), (Kyu-won, et al., 2014), plans for improving efficiency five to tenfold (Weizsacker et al., 2005), designs for sustainable global agriculture (McGill, 2011), forestry (Hansen et al., 2013), and aquaculture (Brugère, 2004) outlines ecological paths forward for sustainability in motion and to manifest the broad interdependence of freedom and community.

A Self-Conscious Symbiont Sutra[27]

Life's history is not just a story of the great improbability. Life reflects a self-organizing proclivity we have just begun to understand, a participatory ability to exchange genetic material even in bacteria, cooperation among individual members of the same species and mutually beneficial symbiosis between different species.

⊡

Symbiosis is a fundamental aspect of sustainability. The cooperative integration of the web of life is basic not secondary. ⊡

Life has meant, for instance, the growth of interconnection on a continental scale of forest fungal mycelium trading nutrients and signaling chemicals between plant and fungus, tying together the roots of the great forest acting as one interconnected and communicative organism.

⊡

Sustainability's power and purpose in its social manifestations will mean the global market and humanity acting as a supportive and signaling self-conscious symbiont with the earth for mutual benefit.

⊡

This self-conscious symbiont will have an ethics, an economics, a politics, a science, and the practice of conservation biology.

The self-conscious symbiont is an evolutionary and social rebuke to the Hobbesian worldview of life being nasty, brutish, and short, and requiring the ordering ministrations of a ruling Leviathan.

The self-conscious symbiont is higher order expression of cooperative action, a new social Darwinism for the 21st century that uses the pursuit of sustainability and new market rules to make humanity's action and economic growth mean ecological improvement.

The self-conscious symbiont weaves supportive global social webs of supportive economic relationships in a zero pollution–zero waste in the pursuit and practice of sustainability.

This is not utopian dreaming, but the expression of profit seeking economic growth conditioned by new market rules and regulations.

Sustainability as social force practices a self-conscious telos in league with Earth and ecosphere.

Sustainability as social force is a further emergent expression of sustainability and self-consciousness.

6

The Venus Project:
A Perfectly Ordered State
Without Markets

Sustainability can be the expression of all political and economic systems, or none of them. Sustainability is dependent upon actions, consequences, and then response.

The countervailing dream to market fundamentalism is a vision to build a perfect, well-ordered state, such as the Venus Project, that plans a future beyond poverty, markets, money, politics, and war. This is a future in engineered and technocratically administered city-states practicing "resource based economies," communities apparently without much we would call freedom. "What is needed," states the Venus project, "is the intelligent management of the world's resources, and a comprehensive and workable arrangement of environmental and social affairs that are in strict accord with existing resources and the carrying capacity of our planet."[28]

Communities apparently will be administered by a technocratic elite in what amounts to a single party city-state. According to the Venus Project, "Simply stated, a resource-based economy utilizes existing resources rather than money and provides an equitable method of distributing these resources in the most efficient manner for the entire population. It is a system in which all goods and services are available without the use of money, credits, barter, or any other form of debt or servitude."

They have detailed and ambitious plans:

> It is far more efficient to build new cities as self-contained systems from the ground up than to restore and retrofit old ones. New cities can take advantage of the latest technologies and be clean, safe, and desirable places to live. In many instances, a circular arrangement will be utilized.
>
> We need a current survey of all available planetary resources. The first experimental city or planning center will conduct a global survey of arable land, production facilities, transportation, technical personnel, population, and all other necessities required for a sustainable culture. This survey will enable us to determine the parameters for global planning for humanizing social and technological development, based on the carrying capacity of Earth and the needs of its people. This can best be accomplished with a constantly updated, computerized model of our planetary resources.

Perhaps the Venus Project is a model utopia for recovery from a post-apocalyptic future. In any case, it is such an apocalypse we aim to prevent.

The Venus project recalls the 19th century Phalanx of French utopian socialist Charles Fourier. Popular in the United States in the 1830s and 1840s, and popularized by newspaperman Horace Greeley and writer Arthur Brisbane, about thirty Phalanx communities based on collective living and cooperative working were founded in the United States, but they ultimately failed through a familiar combination of being under capitalized, struggling to find a fair way of allocating work and money, and a failure of the original vision to find general acceptance.

Nexus of Sustainability and Social Practice Sutra[29]

Sustainability is the assertion of the life force over our self-destructive proclivities and practices.

⊡

Sustainability as social practice ultimately means peace, not war, justice and fairness.

⊡

Sustainability can be the expression of all political and economic systems, or none of them. Sustainability is dependent upon actions, consequences, and then response.

⊡

Worsening storms, floods, droughts, extreme temperatures, melting ice and rising seas as a consequence of climate change can lead to a countervailing and healing human response, sustainability rising.

⊡

Or each catastrophe, each Hurricane Sandy can be soberly noted while we wait, unable to act to change the self-destructive conduct of industrial business as usual and the march of extinction that may include that of our own species as the consequences of our polluting ways.

⊡

The sum of a high waste, high pollution, high-depletion economy in pursuit of high profit is zero. An empty set.

The sum of a zero waste, zero pollution, zero depletion economy in pursuit of high profit is a geometric increase in monetary capital, and a sustainable restoration and growth of natural capital.

7

The Nexus of Freedom and Community: John Rawls or John Stewart Mill?[30]

Sustainability is the practice of a moral ecology, the awareness that our actions have consequence, to guide our relations with people and with the biosphere. Sustainability is the expression and practice off the new Golden rule: Do onto the earth, as the earth will do onto us.

The nexus of freedom and community must become a major focus for the 21st century. Community was too often almost ignored or given short shrift in paradigmatic philosophical works of the 19th and 20th century.

John Rawls' *Theory of Justice*, for example, which examined justice as fairness within the context of a democratic society, despite its many virtues, does not even mention community in the index. For Rawls and his many followers what matters is the independent judgment of individuals negotiating an imagined social contract and subsequently making reasoned decisions within a liberal, democratic order. Rawls' work proved to many people's satisfaction, first, that justice is fairness and, second, that what is fair is most clearly judged by an assumption of an imagined veil of ignorance. This means that people somehow aren't aware of their circumstances and therefore don't know whether or not they will benefit or suffer from a decision, Therefore they can consider consequences logically and honestly without taint of self-interest.

It's drawing room stuff about discussions of the intelligent, the well-mannered and the well-fed. How this order and its community really comes to be, and how it is really maintained, are not questions of major concerns for the philosopher.

But, I submit that a veil of ignorance is not simply a tool for disinterested contemplation. It is also an assertion that a person can be separated not only from self-interest but from community and collective interest. This is absurd. A veil of ignorance may be a useful tool in a thought experiment, but when applied to the effects upon community and its ecological manifestations, it is lifeless and absurd in the sense that the choice to pollute and to poison for profit becomes a matter of acceptable disembodied musings. Hiding behind a veil of ignorance invites catastrophic consequences.

Asking the question "Suppose we poison our children?" in the drawing room should be understood to be on the same level as asking "Suppose we eat our children?" We cannot separate such questions from the community. We all must become aware of what our actions have wrought and will bring upon the community and not just on individuals and their rights.

John Stewart Mill's 1869 essay *On Liberty* offers a very strong statement of the proper relationship between freedom and community that is quite relevant today. While Mill's work is generally embraced as limiting power of the state, he claims that "The only purpose for which power can be rightfully exercised over any member of a civilized community, against his will, is to prevent harm to others. His own good, either physical or moral, is not a sufficient warrant."

It's also clear that for Mill, limits may be imposed in the interest of the well being of others, and, writ large, are in the interest of the society, the community. Mill writes of "positive acts for the benefit of others, which he may rightfully be compelled to perform." These include "any other joint work necessary to the interest of the society of which he enjoys the protection." Ecological protection and sustainable conduct are logical and rational expressions of Mill's understandings of liberty in the 21st century. Mill writes the following:

> [Society may] . . . authorize the subjection of individual spontaneity to external control, only in respect to those actions of each, which concern the interest of other people. If any one does an act hurtful to others, there is a *primâ facie* case for punishing him, by law, or, where legal penalties are not safely applicable, by general disapprobation. There are also many positive acts for the benefit of others, which he may rightfully be compelled to perform; such as, to give evidence in a court of justice; to bear his fair share in the common defense, or in any other joint work necessary to the interest of the society of which he enjoys the protection; and to perform certain acts of individual beneficence, such as saving a fellow-creature's life, or interposing to protect the defenseless against ill-usage, things which whenever it is obviously a man's duty to do, he may rightfully be made responsible to society for not doing. . . . To make any one answerable for doing evil to others, is the rule; to make him answerable for not preventing evil, is, comparatively speaking, the exception. Yet there are many cases clear enough and grave enough to justify that exception.

Mill was not merely avatar of freedom; he was a most insightful commentator on the relationship between freedom and community and of the first importance for action in the 21st century.

Our future lies in a finely crafted and constantly maintained balance between freedom and community, between the one and the many, between finance capital and natural capital.

Ecology Sutra[31]

Sustainability is the practice of a moral ecology, the awareness that our actions have consequences, to guide our relations with people and with the biosphere. Sustainability is the expression and practice of the new Golden rule: Do onto the earth, as the earth will do onto us.

Sustainability is the awareness of the one and of the many; we are both expressions of the biosphere and inhabitants of the biosphere, our father and mother, sibling and child.

Sustainability is certainly informed by a consciousness of the one and the many, of the Tao and the 10,000 things, of the forest and the trees, of the fish and the sea.

Sustainability means acting for seven generations understanding your family will be a member of them, privileging or disparaging none.

Sustainability erects no barriers between humanity and biosphere, between our breath and our atmosphere.

Sustainability is living as if we have only a single Earth.

8

California Leads

*Sustainability as social force practices a self-conscious telos
in league with Earth and ecosphere.*

In April 2015, California announced plans to reduce green house gasses 40 percent by 2030 using solar electricity, wind, geothermal, cogeneration, and high efficiency. Governor Jerry Brown issued an executive order mandating a dramatic reduction in green house gases over just fifteen years.[32]

This is not just talk. In 2014 California installed 4,316 megawatts of solar PV, the equivalent in capacity of more than four large nuclear plants. In comparison to California, North Carolina was second behind California with 396.6 megawatts of PV.

California, like Germany, with a far less favorable climate for solar energy, is a good example that dramatic development of an efficient renewable energy system and saving reduction in greenhouse gases are possible. I remember when Brown was running for president in New Hampshire in 1980 on a strong pro-solar and anti-nuclear platform. He's not new to the issue. His campaign, unfortunately, did not connect well with NH voters at the time. The subsequent twenty-five years have proven that his policies were prescient.

It is the self-serving inertia preached by the fossil fuel industry and their minions, and by technological pessimists like Vaclav Smil who wrote in *Scientific American* an article titled "A Global Transition to Renewable Energy Will Take Many Decades."

According to Smil, "The great hope for a quick and sweeping transition to renewable energy is wishful thinking."[33]

California demonstrates that the future can be now and that renewable energy is the source for the development of the leading industries of the 21st century, to create millions of jobs, billions of profit, and, at the same time, protect and regenerate natural capital.

If solar PV were to grow as it has been for the past thirty years, solar PV should be able to account for all of the US energy needs by 2030. In 2025 this did not seem at all likely to happen. Technological inertia and political opposition makes it more probable, *if* we take the initiative in the United States like California has done, that solar will account for more than 50 percent of US generation by 2050.

This is a political question. Remember, United States industry turned on a dime at the start of WWII and with amazing speed produced the planes and tanks by the hundreds of thousands instead of domestic cars by the millions. But our task now is much more attractive. We need to build the basis for sustainability, prosperity and survival, not weapons of war.

The pessimism of Smil is based on a "realism" locked into the prospects of business and market rules as usual. Smil also ignores the prospects for continental-scale renewable grids and rapidly emerging low-cost battery technology overcoming the intermittency problem of renewables. The sun isn't always out; the wind doesn't always blow. But on a continental scale, wind, solar, hydro, and storage hydro are inherently self-balancing when connected in high-voltage direct current (HVDC) networked grids. When wind, for example, is not blowing in the East, it is in the West. Combine that with distributed storage technologies from batteries, including vehicle to grid (V2G) and vehicle to home (V2H), and we're talking about an energy revolution.

Smil does allow that effective energy storage could be a game changer. At the end of April 2015, Tesla and Solar City announced plans for home battery storage for PV using the Tesla batteries capable of many thousands of charge-discharge cycles whose price will plunge following completion of TESLA's mega battery factory. PV batteries will be aggressively marketed by Solar City, the largest residential PV installer in the United States, and will make more affordable battery storage manufactured by TESLA available to residential, business, and government customers across the United States and in remote communities around the world, according to Solar City Co-founder and Chief Technology Officer Peter Rive.[34]

Elon Musk, TESLA president, and Solar City co-founder made clear the civilization-altering potential of combining affordable and effective energy storage with solar and other renewables. The TESLA batteries are designed not just for residential and small commercial use, but can be built on gigawatt scale (1,000 Mega watts or one billion watts) for utility use.

Ten billion of such devices combined with solar and wind could provide a global 100 percent renewable power system. And, as Musk points out, we produce a new fleet of 10 billion cars and trucks every ten years. The TESLA battery gigafactory is the sign of things and radical energy transformation to come. We should not overlook the batteries of billions of future electric vehicles as serving as billions of point of future electric storage.

The electric vehicle infrastructure in both Vehicle to Home (V2H) and Vehicle to Grid (V2G) configurations is a key part of a future renewable energy-storage regime. V2H is based on plugging your car into home electric system not just to charge, buy, once charged, to provide backup power to the grid when needed.[35]

Home building codes need to mandate both 220-volt or 480-volt power to facilitate relatively quick charging. When electric prices rise it will become economic to provide power to home from plugged in vehicle batteries with sufficient charge levels. V2G configurations are destined to feed power into commercial and industrial installations.

The advantages of such large-scale distributed battery storage combined with distributed PV is that they require less in the construction of continental scale HVD lines to bring renewable power from where it is generated to where it is used. The precise nature of an unfolding renewable future will be a constant process of co-evolution involving technology and economic and political initiatives. The goal is to facilitate a just in time transformation before irreversible climate catastrophe is unleashed.[36]

We are suffering from a crisis of the imagination, a problem encouraged by the resistance of those clinging to business and pollution as usual, driven by the present and future profits they expect to be earned from their polluting ways.

Business, very large business, is beginning to step up to finance and profit from the sustainable renewable future as a prime example of economic growth resulting in ecological improvement. Solar City also announced a one billion dollar fund from Credit Suisse to finance "commercial solar energy systems—including battery storage systems—for businesses, schools and government organizations across the United States."[37]

And, I've participated in webinars in 2015 by NY Sun discussing the rules for New York's large-scale commercial-industrial PV program to install several thousand mega watts of PV that includes incentives for the use of battery backup systems.

The Utility Challenge

The fundamental challenge for existing utilities is their transition from the 20th century model based on a small number of central-station fossil fuel and nuclear plants to a 21st century utility using efficient renewable energy, including an increasing quantity of distributed generation energy. Utilities traditionally make money both from owning large central-station fossil fuel and nuclear plants, and from the sale of this electricity through transmission and distribution networks. A fully integrated traditional utility owns the power plants, the transmission (high voltage) and distribution lines (lower voltage). Typically, today separate companies own the transmission lines and distribution lines, while another company in the electricity competition owns the power plants under retail electric competition. In this model efficiency and redistributed renewables represent a direct threat to profits.

Every kilowatt-hour not generated and transmitted by the utility represents a direct reduction in kilowatt-hour sales and a hit to the bottom line.

Efficiency and renewables are valued in the present model only to the extent they might prevent immediate capital investment needed for overloaded transmission and distribution lines, or perhaps to delay a need to supply power before a new fossil plant is ready, and thereby prevent the purchase of expensive power during the peak hours of use. Hours of high demand require additional and more expensive power plants to provide this peak power. This is frequently fossil-fuel combustion turbines. It could also be renewable power from battery storage, which is more expensive than the cost of generation without storage.

But, as the capital cost of renewables continue to plunge, and since renewables like sun, wind, and hydro have zero fuel costs, traditional utility power will become uncompetitive in retail and wholesale power markets, even if these plants continue to be permitted to pollute without charge. The threat from efficient renewables to business and pollution as usual is that the billions invested in fossil fuel and nukes will become "stranded."

If it's cheaper to buy power from a zero-fuel cost renewable source then from a fossil fuel or nuclear behemoth, the income stream repaying investors in these polluting plants will dry up. This is the so-called "utility death cycle." It's no small matter. The fossil fuel and nuclear infrastructure represent trillions of dollars in invested capital. This is the world's largest agglomeration of capital designed to make money for decades to pay off the original investment and generate a steady profit stream from business and pollution as usual.

We must take steps to rapidly change market rules to make it economic for utilities to be the operators and sponsors of the smart, efficient, and renewable grid using wind, solar, hydro, geothermal, and biomass. Utility profits need to be based on efficient operation of the grid and the transmission and generation and storage of power from both millions of distributed renewable generators as well as from large renewable power stations.

My associate Pentti Aalto has spent many years considering the importance of using a fully loaded price to value all aspects of generation, transmission, and storage and to have that price appropriately influence any decisions to generate or use or store power. All users and all generators who take advantage of the smart, efficient, renewable grid should make appropriate payments for the operation and maintenance of such a grid.

An accurate real-time hourly energy price is the operating signal for energy generators. Increasing prices are the signal for pre-determined computer control to increase generation, to defer or cut back load, or use energy from storage. Decreasing prices are the signal to cut back generation, use cheaper energy for tasks, and increase storage.

Rate structures must fairly compensate utilities for their role in facilitating this process. This is reflected through mechanism such as increasing rates of return on invested capital to reward efficient renewable operation and flattened load curves, where generation and storage is balanced and the need to use expensive peaking plants that operate when demand is high and certainly the use of polluting fossil fuels, is minimized or eliminated.

Such rate recovery can be based on a customer charge indexed to total energy flows in and out of a customer's meter. For example, in a given moment, if there is much less renewable generation then use in the grid, then generators can be rewarded, based on the spot power price for their generation, less a fair payment for distribution and transmission services. On the other hand, if there is much more generation then use, the payment for the power then drops to zero, encouraging the use of on-site storage.

It *may* be necessary to have a step to allow *some* recovery for such stranded costs as part of the fundamental transition to the nature of future utility revenue and conduct in order to accelerate the change to efficient renewable energy

On the other hand, it can certainly be argued that private utilities were taking risks with their investments in exchange for future income and profits, and if the nature of the world turned in another direction, then that's just capitalism.

We do not need to always privatize the profits and socialize the losses. But what's needed is to stop the operation of these polluting monsters as fast as possible, and if a financial settlement to prevent bankruptcy or mitigate losses is needed, and it's politically expeditious to open the road ahead, let's make those deals if necessary.

What is needed is a system where utilities are rewarded for building, strengthening, and maintaining efficient renewable grids with potentially millions of distributed generators and distributed users. Users sometimes put power into the gird and sometimes withdraw power from the grid depending on the economics of operation, which must also account for all costs—including pollution. A fully loaded price will allow computer control to decide when it's economical to generate power, when it's economical to store power, when it's economical to sell power back to grid, and when it's economical to buy power from the grid. The utility should be rewarded and make money for facilitating these operations.

This system can be both much more resistant to blackout because of the number of generators, and be made resistant to cyber attacks and disruptions. For example, by engineering generation and use devices to monitor voltage levels and frequency, the system will automatically perform a number of functions.

When voltage drops, for example, generation will switch on or increase output to maintain voltage. If voltage continues to drop, available storage from battery banks or from electrical vehicles to home (V2H) will be used to put power into grid. If voltage still cannot be maintained, devices that are not crucial will reduce operation including, for example, air conditioning temperature settings will be increased and compressor operation limited to decrease demand. If voltage still continues to drop the home or business may disconnect from the grid and operate in islanded mode that may be a single house, or a neighborhood, or a city depending on existing conditions.

Such homeostatic operation does not depend on messages from utility central, but will take place through computer control algorithms at a speed equal to that of the response of utility automatic generation control (AGC). A number of large fossil fuel power plants are designed to throttle quickly to maintain grid voltage and frequency. Distributed generation and control can use computer control algorithms designed for end users to make choices beforehand to determine, for example, what can and cannot be reduced and how much, such as instant hot water shower heating, before the system is automatically forced to enter islanded mode.

Again, the major challenge here is political and regulatory, to properly incentivize and properly define the role of utilities in the 21st century.

What California Teaches Us

California's success is driven primarily, not simply by favorable sun irradiation, but by conscious choices to facilitate and mandate aggressive pursuit of solar development on an integrated statewide basis. There is a combination of regulatory mandates, planning, and a system of market-driven economic incentives where installers bid on prices for which they are able to install various quantities of PV.

The California Renewable Action Mechanism (RAM), according to the California Utility Commission, "is a simplified market-based procurement mechanism for renewable distributed generation (DG) projects greater than 3 MW and up to 20 MW on the system side of the meter. The Commission adopted RAM as the primary procurement tool for system-side renewable DG because it will promote competition, elicit the lowest costs for ratepayers, encourage the development of resources that can utilize existing transmission and distribution infrastructure, and contribute to RPS goals in the near term."[38]

The feed-in-tariff is a mechanism where PV installers are given a long-term contract at a fixed price determined by the RAM bidding that they can take to the bank to finance their project. "The weighted average of the highest executed contract price from each of the three California utilities for RAM projects is 8.9 cents/kWh. Each individual contract is definitely lower than that . . . and potentially much lower. . . . Some of the world's cheapest solar, is now online and working for ratepayers."[39]

Contract PV prices and subsides drop as the economies of scale and ongoing innovation and experience continues to drive price per watt of photovoltaics progressively downward. This is the PV experience and the power of market forces and renewable technology in action.

At its heart, photovoltaics is a semi-conductor product like computers where efficacy soars while costs plunge. Most broadly, the growth and rise of an efficient renewable future is another expression of the computer and the information age. This is an expression of our times that provides a real savings opportunity for an efficient renewable-energy transformation. If this happens, how it happens, and when it happens depends on the choices and actions of all of us.

9

Solar Energy Threatens Profits of Utilities, Not the Poor

The earth is not a simulacrum of the competitive capitalist market place. Self-destructive industrial capitalism, in fact, is predicated not on natural rhythms and practices, but on creating externalities, the ability to pollute, deplete and destroy without direct cost to the polluter. The polluting market acts as cost shifter making economic growth mean ecological destruction, not ecological improvement.

For investor-owned Tucson Electric in Arizona, solar energy is a threat that calls for them to impose rate hikes and new monthly charges as high as $50.00 a month for any customer who installs solar electricity on their roof.

New charges will make sure everyone "pays their fair share" for maintaining the utility distribution system. Otherwise, the utility would have to raise rates and hurt the poor who can't afford solar. For the suits and their PR guys in Tuscon, solar energy's just another yuppie rip-off.

Or is it?

At Con Edison in New York they are singing a different tune. "Demand for solar is soaring. . . . We will be ready for this change," says Con Ed CEO John McAvoy. "We won't just respond to change. We will lead."[40]

Meanwhile, Pacific Gas and Electric (PG&E), is helping to meet California's goal to slash greenhouse gas emissions 40 percent by 2030 and grow the economy. PG&E is aggressively supporting PV and other renewables, energy efficiency, and making huge investment in charging stations to get more electric cars on the road.[41]

What Con-Ed and PG&E understand is that the successful 21st century electric utility will sell much more energy, not less. Electricity, not gasoline, will power our cars. Electricity, not natural gas and oil, will heat and cool homes through efficient heat pumps.

A 21st century utility will be a smart network ultimately integrating millions of distributed sources of power from solar, wind, and electric car batteries plugged into the system. The 21st utility will earn its money by operating and coordinating the smart and efficient renewable grid, not by selling power from a handful of giant fossil fuel and nuclear plants.

For old time utilities like Tucson Electric with their old time rate incentives, each kilowatt-hour they do not sell is a direct hit to the bottom line.

Millions are now replacing incandescent bulbs with LEDs, using 75 percent less energy. Sales will plunge, and utilities rates will rise if they are based on income from sales, not on efficient use of the distribution system.

The Tucson Electrics of the world haven't the nerve to put out press releases saying that LEDs, which cost more than incandescents, are a threat to the poor, and people who save, should pay a steep monthly surcharge on their bills.

But that's exactly what they are saying about solar energy. Generating a kilowatt on your roof is no different than saving a kilowatt with an LED.

For each kilowatt you don't buy through efficiency improvements, or don't buy because you produced it yourself, the same thing happens. You don't pay the utility for the power or for the cost of delivering it to your home.

Net Metering

Utilities across the country are also digging in their heels against net metering. If your solar system produces more power than you use, it's sold back to the utility at a credit for both the distribution cost and the value of power. Literally or figuratively, the energy you generate spins your electric meter backward.

If the meter literally spun backward or calculated electronically your monthly net use between power purchased or power generated and sold back into the gird, your monthly bill would be reduced by the total amount of electricity produced.

If you produced more energy then you used, your electric bill would be zero, except for the monthly customer charge, and the net metering credit would be carried forward as a credit to next month.

For the old-time utility this is the worst of all worlds. And this is what they are fighting will all their might.

But the truth is that net metering credits are sold back to you at full price by the utility for distribution and energy. The real reduction to the bottom line in a year from net metering is zero. Every kilowatt hour you generate and receive a credit for net metering, you redeem by buying a kilowatt from the utility for the full distribution and energy price.

The real problem is a 20th century revenue model threatened by 21st century renewable, efficiency, and smart-grid technology. The answer for utilities and regulators is what PG&E and California understands—sell more efficient renewable electricity and be able to make money as operator and facilitator of the smart grid.

Sustainability
As Social Force Sutra[42]

Sustainability as social force is about reversing the industrial market path to self-destruction and making economic growth mean ecological improvement.

◎

The earth is not a simulacrum of the competitive capitalist market place. Self-destructive industrial capitalism, in fact, is predicated not on natural rhythms and practices, but on creating externalities, the ability to pollute, and deplete and destroy resources without direct cost to the polluter. The polluting market acts as cost shifter making economic growth mean ecological destruction, not ecological improvement.

◎

The social practice of sustainability is an economic and social aikido redirecting the destructive energy of markets toward constructive and ecologically restorative ends. This is not magic. but the application of comprehensive new market rules and ecological consumption taxation that allows the price system to send clear signals for sustainability, and this makes the pursuit of profit mean ecological improvement and the growth of natural capital.

◎

The global market that pervades all human action, that reaches the most obscure outposts on the earth, must become a restorative and healing force for the ecosphere to manifest conscious humanity's role as global symbiont and planetary trustee guided by an ethics, an economics, a moral ecology, and a conservation biology.

◻

Sustainability as social force might be accomplished as a self-evident imperative combining the practice of enlightened self-interest by governments, and by the rich and the powerful. But, as a global transformative force, sustainability ascendant is most likely to be catalyzed by a great global rising from below demanding restorative change and an end to self-destructive conduct. This great rising from the global commons will mean the thousands in the streets become tens of thousands and become millions demanding the pursuit of survival and shared prosperity.

◻

Sustainability as social force is against the continuation of the path toward ecological self-destruction while embracing the aggressive pursuit of ecological improvement. Any social or economic form can serve to pillage or to sustain. Sustainability, and the devil, is in the details.

◻

Both a global growth market strategy to make economic growth mean ecological improvement and a de-growth strategy for economic contraction and reduction in ecological pillage are options for alternative futures, and both are very difficult challenges.

◦

We must choose a path before the emergent ecological crisis and the prospects of collapse forecloses our options, and, at best, we are forced to embrace dramatic economic contraction in the context of global depression, mass unemployment, social and political instability, resource wars, widening hunger and famine, mass migrations of the desperate, epidemics, rising seas, and collapsing agriculture, aquaculture, fisheries, and forestry.

◦

If humanity continues to pursue the path of industrial self-destruction we will arrive at some dystopian version of a Mad Max future. What happens is rooted, in part, in our response to the opportunity and to the clear and present danger.

◦

Humanity's role, by necessity, and conscious action, must be transformed from that of self-destructive parasite to supportive global symbiont.

10

Greenhouse Gases: What's Sustainable and Who's Responsible?

As an afterthought, it seems, the earth and ecosphere will do quite well without us as a sustainable system . . . unless we somehow manage to irredeemably destroy the ability of organisms to transform carbon dioxide into oxygen.

The current *average* annual, global carbon dioxide that is released as a result of human activities is 4.5 tons per person per year. Unfortunately, only an amount of three tons per person, based on a global carbon allowance for 7 billion people, keeps atmospheric carbon dioxide at stable levels. This discrepancy between 3.0 tons person and 4.5 tons per person average is what is driving climate change.

The central goal on a global level is to reduce total carbon to 3 tons per person per year. This means it is essential to develop efficient renewables to replace fossil fuels, in addition to reducing carbon and other GHG emissions from cement and concrete, reducing methane from industrialized animal feedlots, and increasing the GHG removal capacity of soil, grasslands, and biomass.

At 3.0 tons per person per year, carbon added by human activity for 7 billion of us equals the approximately 20 gigatons of natural carbon sinks of ocean and soil and biomass (+/- 4.6 gigatons).[43]

In 2004-13 annual global carbon releases were about 35.9 gigatons. This means that after the sinks, the atmospheric carbon increased annually by about 15.8 gigatons a year.[44]

A seven billion population meeting an average 3.0 tons per year carbon allowance would mean about annual carbon of 21 gigatons per year, roughly equal to the natural carbon sinks and therefore in a long-term sustainable balance.

Reducing global carbon this amount per person does not, however, address already existing emissions and their consequences. Stable emissions need be combined with a global cooling regime that can, for example, remove huge amounts of carbon through reforestation, proper grassland management for grazing, and hydrothermal carbonization (HTC) for the production of biocoal for *terra preta* soil enrichment, and proper agro-forestry for desert cultivation.[45] The goal is to remove 200 gigatons of carbon over the next 30 years to reduce atmospheric carbon to the sustainable 330 ppm range.

Current National Carbon Emissions

National per capita carbon emissions vary enormously and fluctuate yearly, as shown in the data from the following countries:[46]

> Qatar: 36.9 tons
>
> United States: 17.3 tons
>
> Australia: 17.0 tons
>
> Russia: 11.6 tons
>
> Germany: 9.3 tons
>
> UK: 7.8 tons
>
> China: 5.4 tons
>
> India: 1.4 tons
>
> Africa average: 0.9 tons
>
> Ethiopia: 0.1 tons

Carbon Dioxide Imbalance Under Business as Usual

There is some inconsistency in various reports of carbon data. This can be a result of a combination of exactly what is counted and how, what year's data are included in each summary, what years are included in latest national reports, and annual fluctuations. The relative comparisons between emitters, however, are consistent. The best data is available using the ODIAC data set from the NOAA Earth System Research Laboratory in Boulder, Colorado.

More importantly, global totals are reflected in the accurate NOAA Mana Loa Observatory weekly measurements of atmospheric carbon dioxide. For the week beginning February 1, 2015, the measurement was 400.21 ppm, up from 397.92 ppm one year ago in 2014, and 379.40 ppm ten years ago in 2005. This is real data, and the basis, unless we act, for ecological catastrophe.[47]

This measurement is the irrefutable basis for the science behind climate change. There can be disagreements about the speed and precise nature of the ecological consequences that will overwhelm us if carbon dioxide is inexorably allowed to continue to increase in the atmosphere and continue to dissolve in water and acidify the oceans.

But the fundamental truth is the accurately measured quantity of carbon dioxide in the atmosphere. The relationship between global climate change and increasing atmospheric and oceanic carbon dioxide concentrations is not just theory, but fundamental to the geological record.

Past Carbon Dioxide Emissions

China and developing nations point to the historic responsibility for GHG emissions of the advanced industrial states. Summary historical GHG emissions data, as of 2005, is given as the following:

1. US: 339,174 megatons (MT) GHG or 28.8 percent
2. Germany, UK, France: 186,624 MT or 15.47 percent
3. China: 105,915 MT or 9.0 percent
4. Russia: 94,679 MT or 8.0 percent
5. Japan: 45,629 MT or 3.87 percent
6. India: 28,824 MT or 2.44 percent
7. Canada: 25,716 MT or 2.2 percent
8. Ukraine: 25,431 MT or 2.2 percent[48]

China: Global Warming Emissions and Renewable Development

China, while emerging as the global factory, and largest greenhouse gas emitter, has become a world leader in photovoltaic and wind production, having installed 7 gigawatts of wind in 2014 compared to about 3 gigawatts installed in United States.[49]

China installed 3.2 gigawatts solar electric in the first half of 2014, more than their total in 2013, compared to a United States total in 2014 of about 2.5 gigawatts solar.[50]

A significant portion of China's emissions are a consequences of production exported to the West. When accounting for these "consumption" emissions, EU emissions have appear to have stabilized, but, according to the Global Carbon Project, would be 30 percent higher if we accounted for those goods that are produced elsewhere.[51]

China has undertaken initiatives to reduce greenhouse gas intensity by 40-45 percent from their 2005 level by 2020.[52] China replaced traditional GDP accounting with ecologically nuanced measures[53] and accepted reduced growth rates and sound development as the new normal.[54]

The recent presidential agreements between China and the United States are the beginnings of an effective greenhouse gas plan. President Barack Obama said the move was "historic" as he set a new goal of reducing the levels of the United States to between 26 percent–28 percent by 2025, as compared with 2005 levels. President Xi Jinping did not set a specific China target, but indicated emissions would peak by 2030. (according to the BBC, 2014).[55]

The latest review of China's progress on carbon dioxide from the Grantham Research Institute of the London School of Economics (LSE) in 2015 suggests that China's emissions are likely to peak by 2025, if not before, and may be followed by ongoing and significant reductions. The conclusions from the LSE on China's new development path is a message of global hope and just-in-time deliverance:

> Were China's emissions indeed to peak around 2020–2025, it would be reasonable to expect a peak emissions level for China of around 12.5–14 billion tonnes of carbon dioxide equivalent. This could hold open the possibility that global GHG emissions could be brought onto a pathway consistent with the international goal of limiting global warming to no more than 2°C. Whether the world can get onto that pathway in the decade or more after 2020 depends in significant part on China's ability to reduce its emissions at a rapid rate, post-peak (as opposed to emissions plateauing for a long time), on the actions of other countries in the next two decades, and on global actions over the subsequent decades.[56]

The questions remain: Will the United States and China make the basic choices and the necessary investments to eliminate fossil fuel pollution with efficient renewables and leave fossil fuels in the ground if they cannot be used without causing pollution? Will the United States and China help lead the world toward a global sustainable carbon allowance of 3.0 tons carbon per person per year? It's a global challenge that **we all must** successfully, fairly, and creatively respond to. All of us must converge on a sustainable global carbon budget.

Sustainability as Enchantment, Not Reduction, Sutra

Sustainability means redefinition and reconceptualization of both abstract and concrete industrial categories, behaviors, and productive processes transformed in accord with ecological norms. Sustainability is characterized by enchantment, not reduction.

◌

Sustainability as social practice means acting in response to inescapable necessity, actions that take place just in time.

◌

Sustainability is economic and social wellspring for entrepreneurship and cultural creativity and creation.

◌

Sustainability is inherently imprecise. It addresses the interpenetration of the ecosphere and civilization, conditioned, as all living creatures are, by the health of the ecosphere.

◌

Civilization's actions represent a self-conscious expression of a second nature with powers and destructive consequences that have transcended ordinary biological constraints. Epistemology now redefines ontology.[57]

◌

The rhythms of the ecosphere, in accord with the processes of Gaea, seem to tend toward the homeostatic and therefore the sustainable. But the history of life, and therefore of the ecosphere and of sustainability, is a history of periodic mass extinctions and life's recovery. It is a score with glottal stops and changes in rhythm and key.

As an afterthought, it seems, the earth and ecosphere will do quite well without us as a sustainable system—unless we somehow manage to irredeemably destroy the ability of organisms to transform carbon dioxide into oxygen.

Sustainability walks astride the fence between biosphere and social sphere, balancing as if standing first on one foot, then the other, performing the White Stork Kicks Up Qui Gong pose.[58]

Sustainability is a property of the ecosphere reflecting a process of ceaseless change moving at different rates of speed that inevitably has led to the evolution and extinction of species as fungible expressions of the biota.

Sustainability is the dynamic resolution of the contradiction between biological and social change.

Sustainability as both biological and social process is more than the sum of its parts. It's possibilities and limits tend toward the practice of an ecological nano-technology and of Dharma Gaea.

⊡

Sustainability is both art and science. As art, it is protean, creating ever-new expressions and surprising juxtapositions; as science, it is the expression of an irreducible dynamism, a state conditioned by its parts, but representing a grand, ultimately homeostatic, dynamics.

⊡

Sustainability can be applied to the biological community, and to a drop of water, and to Gaea as a whole and beyond, extending to a universe of space-time, matter-energy, consequence, and consciousness.

⊡

Sustainability is the physical and spiritual expression of the summary equations describing the ecosphere in motion.

⊡

Sustainability as a process inextricable from homeostasis is one state of human consciousness with its requisite retinue of mood and mean, tragedy and comedy.

11

What Can Happen?

Is sustainability, the manifest force behind an evolutionary and universal direction, time's one-way arrow toward self-consciousness, not limited to the bounds of the Earth, but generalized throughout the universe?

We've broken the 400 parts per million carbon dioxide in the atmosphere. What happens if humanity continues to pour more and more carbon dioxide into the atmosphere and into the oceans?

If fossil fuel pollution continues to pour more and more carbon dioxide into the atmosphere we risk a replay of the Paleocene-Eocene Thermal Maximum (PETM) of 55 million years ago, risking a very likely catastrophic end to global civilization.

The PETM lasted 200,00 years before the excess carbon was removed from the atmosphere.

This is the potential consequences of the continuation along the business as usual industrial path to self-destruction.

Scientists studying the PETM conclude:

> The Paleocene/Eocene thermal maximum. . . . was a brief [200,000 year] period of widespread, extreme climatic warming . . . associated with massive atmospheric greenhouse gas input. . . . sea surface temperatures near the North Pole increased from ~18 °C to over 23 °C during this event. Such warm values imply the absence of ice and thus exclude the influence of ice-albedo feedbacks on this Arctic warming. At the same time, sea level rose while anoxic and euxinic

conditions developed in the ocean's bottom waters and pho-
tic zone . . . the absolute polar temperatures that we derive
before, during and after the event are more than 10°C warmer
than those model-predicted.[59]

We are courting the release of global forces that will act on a
geological time scale, and can persist for longer than homo sapiens
have existed as a species.

Sustainability and Time's One-Way Arrow Sutra

Is sustainability limited to the conduct of one planet's ecosphere?

⊡

It is presumptuous to assume that the limits to sustainability's influence are the limits of a particular ecosphere defined by the fuzzy boundary between atmosphere and space and living subsoil and the rock below.

⊡

Is sustainability, the manifest force behind an evolutionary and universal direction, time's one-way arrow toward self-consciousness, not limited to the bounds of the earth, but generalized throughout the universe?[60]

⊡

Einstein's relativity was informed by his insight of the consequences that physical law governing matter, energy, space, and time operated the same in all frames of reference whether we are on a space station moving close to the speed of light, and breathing our reproduced atmosphere and feeling gravity produced through slow revolution, or walking on planet Earth as it revolves and hurtles through space.

⊡

Sustainability and the movement toward mind and self-consciousness is similarly another physical law of universal applicability, of theme and endlessly created variation in response to different circumstance. Sustainability is therefore the particular creating the general.

◌

Sustainability is also evidentiary. It is process as well as historical record.

◌

Sustainability represents a definitive refutation of the concept of the billiard ball universe of particles crashing into one another, where, given a complete knowledge of existing conditions, the future is predictable, save for the operation of chance quantum prospects, and time can be run, in principle, both forward and backward.

◌

Sustainability is the track not of particles in a bubble chamber, but of the emergent self-conscious universe, a qualitative departure from the mechanistic world, the complexity of complexities quickening and reflecting and re-shaping.

◌

Sustainability is shaped by physical law and enlivened by self-consciousness.

◌

The fact that action is very much a product of circumstances and collective influence is a key reflection of sustainability, and not a rejection of self-conscious choice and its influence. Reality, the co-evolved being, and contingency, the unpredictable and the surprising and emergent present, conditions and guides our actions and choices.

◻

Sustainability is experience attested by our survival, manifest not only in our genes but in the nature of the ecosphere in all its aspects and in all its future potentials and implications.

◻

Sustainability is the creation of nested and interpenetrating wholes that are more than the sum of their and our parts.

◻

Sustainability should call forth wonder and reverence not the arrogance of the abuse of our power.

◻

Sustainability's course is shaped by physical law enlivened by self-consciousness and creativity whose ultimate bounds can scarcely be envisioned or parsed. Sustainability in many ways is the province of limitless limits.

◻

Universal physical law and its ethical manifestation in human self-consciousness can, as an integral part of sustainability, act in a healing social response to industrial excess. Sustainability in action does not, by itself mean a timely and civilization saving end to the mad pursuit of industrial ecologically self-destructive conduct.

◻

Sustainability can be understood as a 21st Newtonian law of social mechanics, the course of industrial self-destruction redirected and re-formed by sustainability's outside social force.

⊡

Sustainability in restorative social action is the self-conscious manifestation of billions of years of the evolution and mind. It is the logical co-evolutionary response to the unfolding ecological consequences of industrial pollution.

⊡

Sustainability is a stunning self-conscious application of the second law of thermodynamics where intent adds energy to the system to help provide order out of chaos.

⊡

Sustainability in action means simply that we must re-form the nature of our actions and their consequences.

⊡

Sustainability does not mean that we must change ourselves and always follow our better angels. It does not mean an attempt to banish greed, or vanity, or selfishness. The pursuit of sustainability means the creation of social structures that facilitate the pursuit of sustainable ends.

⊡

In this fashion Marx was right in understanding, after the fact, that the economic system could be found to be determining and supporting the philosophical and political superstructure. The pursuit of sustainability in motion means the co-evolution and co-determination of the economic, the political, the philosophical, the social, the technological for ecological improvement.

Sustainability means an end to business and pollution as usual. Sustainability does not choose in the abstract any particular social or economic system. For us it means that economic growth must mean ecological improvement.

12

Paths to a Sustainable Future

A category error is to consider all of economic growth inherently self-destructive, instead of reflecting its specific conduct and effects. A society of tender service and industrial ecology can certainly be dynamic, profitable, and sustainable. Indeed it must be.

Before we turn to examining transformative means to help build a prosperous and just global ecological future, such as the Basic Energy Entitlement (BEE) and Basic Income Guarantee (BIG) that we will consider below in other sections, I want to lead us through a brief examination of what it means for us to follow an ecological path. This will help put the BIG, the BEE, and other measures such as Ecological Assessments and Advanced Energy Performance Contracting in context of a part of much broader changes.

While following an ecological path will mean much change from business and pollution as usual, it is far from a bitter pill. It is designed to create a sustainable ecological world that is prosperous, healthy, peaceful, and just.

Our path to a sustainable future must engage four basic and mutually supportive and interactive realms to move an industrial business as usual to an ecological future. It's crucial to understand that all of these measures are both clearly possible and firmly within the grasp of existing institutions. This pathway to an ecological future can be grasped and pursued by all of us and become part of our daily lives, our jobs, our businesses, our communities.[61]

Four Interactive Realms

The ecological pie can be understood to have four basic and interactive realms.

1. Economic
2. Political
3. Technical
4. Philosophical

Each realm has a number of attributes, and each realm, most crucially, has a communicative, or cybernetic, feedback relationship with the other realms.

Key Dynamics of an Ecological Global Growth Agenda

1. *Economic*
Economic growth means ecological improvement and regeneration of natural capital.

2. *Political*
New market rules and ecological assessments should crafted to send clear price signal for sustainability.

3. *Technical*
Build the zero waste, zero pollution productive infrastructure for energy, industry, mining, agriculture, forestry, and aquaculture.

4. *Philosophical*
Build foundation for global peace and justice through mechanisms like Basic Income Guarantee (BIG) and Basic Energy Entitlement (BEE) as manifestation of enlightened self-interest that benefits all.

The intent of an ecological global growth agenda is expansion of markets and reduction of pollution, resource depletion, and ecological damage. It is a recipe for more jobs, healthier communities, and building a global structure for peace and ecological justice. It means leaving no one behind or left out.

Snapshots of an Ecological Global Growth Agenda

An ecological global growth agenda is focused on reversing the connection between economic growth and ecological pillage. It means pollution-free renewable energy, and leaving fossil fuels in the ground it they cannot be used without ecologic damage. It means increasing efficiency of operations by a factor of five or ten and similarly reducing material inputs.

It means production through use of 3-D printing with sustainable inputs and production where all outputs become inputs for other processes. It means an agriculture resulting in soil building as well as food production and global cooling by removing carbon from the atmosphere. It means a forestry resulting in an increase in biomass and reduction in atmospheric carbon dioxide.

In general terms, the dynamic of ecological improvement and regeneration of natural capital must apply to any productive activity human activity whether through markets, or voluntary exchange based on use values, or determined by planning and administered prices.

The everyday lives in an ecological future are based on a shared sense of ecological justice and fairness that helps provide the basis for a common awareness of and an existential security. An "ecological civilization" is a society whose everyday lives are more than just for material gain and to put food on the table, but also a part of the work of healing nature and striving for ecological justice and fairness.

This is accomplished not because we all suddenly listed to our better angels, but because we have established and maintained social, political, and economic mechanisms that send clear signals for sustainable economic growth, ecological improvement, and ecological justice. Increased quarterly profits in an ecological future are structured to also mean ecological improvement and meeting obligations for social justice.

An Ecological Market Sutra

A category error is to consider all of economic growth inherently self-destructive, instead of reflecting its specific conduct and effects. A society of tender service and industrial ecology can certainly be dynamic, profitable, and sustainable. Indeed it must be.

◦

Sustainability is the embrace of limits and ecological market rules as protective boundaries facilitating constructive, transformative acts.

◦

Sustainability is the empowerment of ecological transformation.

◦

Sustainability is the high profit center for the 21st century and beyond.

◦

Sustainability is the condition necessary for the continuation of economic growth, profit, and human prosperity.

◦

Sustainability is the optimizing the three bottom lines of sustainability for human action—the economic, the ecological, the social.

◦

Sustainability ultimately must encompass all human acts. It is, at the micro and macro levels, the activity and health of the ecosphere.

13

A Chinese Ecological Path

Sustainability acting in creative response to all influences is an ever-evolving practice, more process and principle based then rule based.

China is attempting to emerge as global leader, both in word and in deed, in transforming industrial business and pollution as usual to an ecological civilization. The success of these efforts, and our common future, hangs in the balance.

China has enormous ecological problems that it recognizes as the basis for comprehensive ecological reform. As the global factory, for China to aggressively pursue a zero waste and zero pollution circular economy is crucial for solution of the ecological problems of the Anthropocene. It is necessary for China to pursue an ecological path for a global ecological civilization to emerge; it is not sufficient, of course, for China to act alone. China has become, however, a major player in this drama.

China's GDP economic growth has been phenomenal in the last thirty-five years, from GDP of 364.5 billion yuan ($59 billion US dollars) in 1978 to 56,900 billion yuan in 2014 ($9.4 trillion dollars), making the China the world's second largest economy.

The April 25, 2015 policy blueprint on building what they term an ecological civilization approved by the CPC Central Committee and State Council can be, in retrospect, be seen as a key step in China's avowed pursuit of a sustainable ecological future that will accept a reduced rate of economic growth in exchange for ecological improvement.[62]

First, the policy blueprint recognizes "serious environmental pollution, ecological degradation . . . restricting sustainable economic and social development." Second, it details nine areas in pursuit of explicit ecological development policies. The blueprint is serious in intent. It follows on the heels of a March 2015 technical policy document that explored these issues.

In essence, the blueprint commits Party and government to go all-in, on all levels, as "the powerful force of ecological civilization construction." There is to be "zero tolerance" for ecological violations, and the establishment of ecological "red lines."

Two blueprint themes stood out. First, is the embrace of a circular economy and the development of green industry. Under a circular economy, nothing is wasted. All outputs at all stages of product's life cycle become inputs for other processes. The air, water, and land is no longer a sink for pollution and poison.

To help make this real, it's time for China to establish a well-capitalized Ecological Development Bank (EDB) with a clear ecological mission. This was proposed in 2015 by researchers from China's Central Bank.[63] Similarly, the new China led Asia Infrastructure and Investment Bank (AIIB) should be governed by green mandates.[64]

Second, is the question of carbon reduction. China, despite its leadership position in PV and wind energy, and now High Voltage Direct Current (HVDC) transmission, is still committed to coal. Efficiency improvements are planned using Super Critical and Ultra Critical coal plants, leading to a peaking of carbon by 2030 and then reductions.

I am not confident that China and the world have the time for this plan before negative ecological changes overwhelm us. Building a "strong and smart gird" for China should take full advantage of the ability to move renewable power and stored electricity over long distances using HVDC from where it's generated to where it is needed.[65]

Good news is reflected in the report in 2015 *China's New Normal* by the Grantham Research Institute of the London School of Economics (LSE) that states China's emissions are likely to peak by 2025, if not before, and will be followed by ongoing and significant reductions under China's plans for the future. China in word and deed is choosing to condition economic growth by ecological consequences.[66]

The question, of course, for all of us is to what extent, and at what speed, will plans on a local, national, and global level become reality. Will ecological policy and practices change happen quickly enough before the consequences of rising temperatures, rising seas, drought and flood, and crop failure foreclose our options?

That China's astounding economic rise as global factory was based on the practice of industrial business and pollution as usual is clear. What is not as clearly understood is that China is attempting to turn the page toward sustainable growth and to act as a leader in global markets in ecological technologies of the 21st century.

While many in American leadership are largely lawyers by training, like Barack Obama, the Chinese leadership are overwhelmingly engineers and scientists and economists and practical men.

The top four members of the current Politburo Standing Committee includes President Xi Jinping, who studied chemical engineering at Tsinghua University in Beijing; Premier Li Keqiang has a PhD in economics; Vice-Premier Zhang Dejiang has a degree in economics; Yu Zhengsheng, Chairman of the Chinese People's Consultative Congress, graduated from Harbin Military Engineering Institute and specialized in missile design. We can hope these men put their technical skills to good ends and turn good words into ecological good deeds in an ongoing basis.

14

China's Ecological Pivot: A Report from the World Cultural Forum

Sustainability is a reflection of and proof for the existence of a fundamental ethics and ethical principles.

The second World Cultural Forum held in Hangzhou, China, in 2013, witnessed what may be, in retrospect, the start of an epochal pivot by the Chinese leadership toward a balanced and productive ecological future.[67]

The 500-person conference, with a mix of Chinese and international invitees, made it explicit that China and the rest of the world need to take aggressive steps to restore ecological harmony and balance. The common understanding was that the hour is late and much must be done. An ecologically balanced civilization is not merely the aspiration of social theorists and professors.

Where the forum departed from the usual litany of ecological woes, threats, and solutions was that there were people present who had the power to help realize these changes. Senior Chinese officials explicitly recognized the need to embrace a reduction in the rate of growth for the sake of ecological improvement, and the Hangzhou Declaration, approved by the conference, calls for a global commitment to building an "ecological civilization." Chaired by Yu Zhengsheng of the Chinese People's Political Consultative Congress (a Politburo member and the fourth-most powerful politician in China), the conference did not pull punches.

The Hangzhou Declaration

Ecological civilization is a new civilization form that is beyond industrial civilization. Its core concept is to respect, comply with and preserve nature; it is based on the carrying capacity of resources and the environment, takes natural laws as guiding principles and regards sustainable development as the aim; it fundamentally changes the traditional mode of production and way of life featuring excessive consumption of natural resources and excessive waste emissions; it develops green economy, circular economy and low carbon economy, constructs a resource-saving and environment-friendly society, promotes the harmonious coexistence of human and nature and the harmonious development of human and society. It is not only the highest priority in responding to global ecological crisis, but also the long-term plan for the progress of human civilization.[68]

I was asked by the organizers to prepare a plenary speech detailing a business-centered approach to ecological change supported by government leadership. I defined an ecological civilization as one where economic growth means ecological improvement.[69] The business value proposition to drive the transition is that we can extract profits from the trillions of dollars currently spent on fossil fuels and related infrastructure.

A Twenty-Year Plan for Transformation

I outlined to the plenary several policy tools that could drive a twenty-year transformation to renewable energy—a crucial, but clearly not sufficient, linchpin of any good ecological future:

⊚ Mandate an increasing percentage of renewable energy generation and storage on continental, regional, and local scales as relevant; at the same time, mandate conversion of coal to zero emissions or leave it in the ground with all current coal subsidies redirected to emissions reductions. The capital cost of renewable generation continues to decrease rapidly, and it is already dramatically cheaper to save a kilowatt of energy than it is to generate one. Requiring that an escalating percentage of energy be supplied by renewables would catalyze further cost reductions.[70]

◎ Advanced Energy Performance Contracting on a utility scale, combining renewable energy revenues and efficiency savings, could finance mass retrofits on the city and utility level through market capital. These would be competitively bid by installation contractors on a mass scale with revenues obtained from utility rates. This is a means of building the renewable energy future without any tax increases and a means of reducing long-term energy bills.[71]

◎ Impose severance taxes or resource royalties on all energy consumed, or mined/extracted, to build permanent sovereign funds for global investment in sustainability. The world should not be divided between a rich minority living in relative ecological and economic security, and a poor majority suffering from ecological and economic deprivation. The use of severance taxes on natural capital, undertaken by the Norway Oil Fund and Alaska Permanent Fund, is a logical way to raise revenue for ongoing capital investment in efficient renewables for the poor. Severance taxes should be imposed on both polluting and depleting fossil energy resources, as well as on renewables obtained from the global commons be it the sun, wind, or hydro.

◎ Establish a Global Basic Energy Entitlement (BEE) of 70 gigajoules (19,443 kWh) and 3.0 tons of CO_2 per person per year. Rich nations are far above this standard, while the global poor are not. Fees paid for excess energy use through small assessments on utility bills (about one cent per kWh) called Sustainability Assessments for Valuing the Ecosphere (SAVE) could be used to help capitalize Permanent Sovereign Funds to be invested in sustainable development for the poor, administered by the United Nations or on a country-by-country basis. Income from BEE investments can be used to help fund a BIG or Basic Income Guarantee.

◉ Establish a Global Initiative for Climate Cooling (GICC) to develop mechanisms and market rules to facilitate sustainable investments in energy, cooperating with SAVE and Permanent Funds. The Global Initiative for Climate Cooling would catalyze sustainable development at all levels, from the local to the national and global, by developing appropriate market mechanisms and market rules to help finance the renewable energy transformation.[72]

One example would be developing model energy hedge instruments between energy users and energy developers that benefit both parties. A twenty-year renewable hedge would allow energy developers to obtain an assured and adequate long-term income stream to facilitate market finance, while an energy user, for example, a consortium of institutions or housing complexes, would assure long-term reasonable energy costs with zero capital expense.[73]

In sum, enormous economic and ecological advantage will flow to those who develop low-cost and low-pollution energy. We can make the price system work to send signals for sustainability. For example, sustainable goods and services will gain market share and become more profitable if countries adopt ecological consumption taxes, such as an ecological Value-Added Tax. VAT is already one of China's leading revenue sources.

Hangzhou as an Example of the Ecological Challenge

The city of Hangzhou is renowned in China for its beauty. Tree-lined avenues flow around the iconic West Lake with its classic buildings. It is a sister city of Boston. At the same time, the streets are packed with cars, more and more every week. It took two hours to drive ten miles from the airport in rush hour traffic worse than Boston, and an hour back to the airport on a Sunday. Towering construction cranes are ubiquitous. The air, of course, is no longer pristine.

The Chinese leadership understands the global and domestic ecological crises and has the political power to implement long-term plans. The astounding rise of China as a global economic power is a reflection of this. And so is the rise of China as the current global carbon emissions leader, and as a customer of US coal exports. At the same time, China is the leader in solar photovoltaic production and solar hot water use. Its per capita energy consumption remains low compared to the United States, though its historic contribution to total emissions is fast catching up at current rates.

The Chinese leaders I met with were willing to look at this reality and make appropriate changes. The sentiment was shared by one of the forum organizers, Ervin Laszlo, an eminent European scholar, two-time Nobel Peace Prize nominee, and founder of the Club of Budapest. Lazlo felt that the embrace of the program I presented was an enormously hopeful sign.

The WCF made clear that harmony and balance, both social and ecological, is deeply in accord with Chinese tradition. China may morph once again, from industrial to ecological leader, over the next few decades. If China succeeds in making an ecological turn, the implications will be profound. It also raises the question: If China leads, will the United States follow?

In 2013 it seemed while the industrial machine still roared, that an ecological spring might be blooming in the east. In 2015

China's subsequent policy shifts and faster than expected progress on reducing carbon dioxide emissions are encouraging.

We all await what happens next in China and in the United States, the global economic leaders of the industrial machine, with great interest. I must note that there is no climate denier in control of the Chinese People's Political Consultative Congress. In Beijing, Yu Zhengsheng, who also led the Hangzhou Declaration meeting, is Chair of the Congress. In Washington, the Speaker of the House is John Boehner, loyal servant of his climate-change-denier Republican majority, which aspires to gain control of the presidency, as well, in 2016.

In 2015 we could expect more help in a constructive response to ecological crisis from Yu Zhengsheng in Beijing than from John Boehner in Washington. Strange, isn't it.

PLENARY ADDRESS:

Ecological Civilization World Cultural Forum, Hangzhou, China

Roy Morrison, May 18, 2013

I am honored to be asked to address the Plenary session on building an ecological civilization.

We are in the midst of an epochal transition in human civilization. A new civilization, an ecological civilization, is emerging from within the context of industrial business as usual.

Our century, the 21st century, offers the opportunity for humanity to build day by day, place by place an ecological civilization—a world that is sustainable, prosperous, peaceful, harmonious, and just for all, not just for the fortunate fraction that constitute the rising affluent. A sustainable world cannot be divided between the polluting rich minority and a desperate poor majority.

An ecological civilization will mean a global convergence upon sustainable norms for all in energy, emissions, resources, and natural capital. This process of convergence will help us build sustainability's global infrastructure, transfer resources and knowledge from rich to poor, and establish the economic framework for enduring property. Convergence is not a matter of charity. A sustainable convergence will make us all better off by expanding global wealth, trade, and social contacts manyfold.

An ecological civilization, as working definition, means that economic growth results in ecological improvement. An ecological civilization means decoupling the industrial equation of economic growth with pollution, depletion, and ecological damage. This ecological civilization uses market rules and the price system to send signals for sustainability through ecological consumption taxation and related means to shape consumption, production, and investment decisions. Sustainable goods and services become more profitable and gain market share while inspiring the rapid transformation of polluters. An ecological civilization means far more than no limit to trade in information in a renewably powered cyberspace.

We can build, if we choose to, a global civilization characterized by efficient renewable energy technologies; an industrial ecology with zero waste and zero pollution, where the output of one process becomes the input for another; a world of sustainable agriculture, forestry, and aquaculture by a global cyberspace and marketplace trading in information; and a civilization where industrial production becomes the customized output of 3-D printers using sustainable inputs.

This is a transition that cannot wait for consensus decisions from United Nations climate conferences. An ecological civilization will arise as an expression of a global movement for change. It can and must be undertaken on all levels, by the firm, the family, the neighborhood, the city, the region, the nation, and beyond.

This will mean, all at once, global movements for climate justice, and movements for building an efficient renewable energy infrastructure, new market rules making the price system send clear signals for sustainability, and an overall improvement in efficiency and decrease in waste by orders of magnitude. These movements must involve all of us and demands our participation using all our skills.

Our fundamental challenges are political, not technical. We have the tools and we have the knowledge. But do we have the political will? An ecological civilization cannot be built to privilege historic polluters by imposing restraint upon the newly developed, and likewise must rest upon fair burden sharing by all.

The enormous and self-destructive powers of industrial reality have posed a stark choice. We can continue to follow the path of short-term profit and long-term ruin. We have to all appearances subdued and humbled nature. But that is an illusion if we continue to fell the forests, pour poison into the air, water, and soil; or if we sweep the sea of fish, drain the aquifers, obliterate wild habitat, change the climate, acidify the ocean, and bring about a tidal wide of death and extinction for a large fraction of the world's species, perhaps including our own.

We have a choice not to have a future characterized by deepening ecological catastrophe of drought and flood, of famine, war, epidemic, mass migration of the desperate, of collapsed states, a world of the ghost cities of Peking, New York, Paris, Rio, Johannesburg, and Mumbai reduced to be the only home of the desperate who remain.

And while we may agree on the absolute necessity for action, how do we build the road as we travel from an industrial present to an ecological civilization?

The second great illusion of industrial civilization, beyond equating economic growth with pollution, is that the nations or firms that go first in taking fundamental steps toward sustainability will be at a disadvantage, and thus believe that the transition away from fossil fuels and high pollution will be a net cost instead of an enormous benefit. I will focus here on energy, my area of expertise and a crucial step in ecological transformation.

In fact, the trillions spent on fossil fuels, and the trillions of energy and material wasted, represent an enormous profit center to help drive the global efficient renewable energy transformation and the industrial ecology revolution. How can it still be called "economic" to squander trillions on depleting fossil fuels with wildly fluctuating prices, trillions on the infrastructure to produce and burn them, and further trillions in costs becoming monetized by allowing businesses to engage in "pollution for free" without regard to true expense?

The business proposition for ecological change is to extract savings from the trillions spent on fossil fuels and infrastructure and help finance the efficient renewable infrastructure for a zero fuel cost-zero polluting and sustainable future.

The transition to efficient renewable resources and storage on a continental scale can economically and effectively meet all our energy needs, and can be accomplished largely through the use of market based mechanisms that mine the savings obtained through performance contracting means by combining savings from efficiency and renewable resources to produce savings streams that enable market finance.

Four steps to drive a twenty-year global energy transformation:

First, is to require over twenty years both an increasing percentage of renewable generation to replace polluting generation, and require conversion within twenty years of coal to zero emissions. Coal must be ecologically benign or stay in the ground. All fossil fuel subsidies to be used for zero-emissions development.

Using Advanced Energy Performance contracting on a utility scale combining renewable generation revenues with efficiency savings can finance mass retrofits on city wide and utility scale.

Second, is use of severance taxes on all energy to build Permanent sovereign funds for global investment in sustainable development.

Third, is establishing a sustainable per capita global energy allowance of 70 giga joules (19,443 KWh) of primary energy and three tons of CO_2. Those above the allowance will pay a small tax on their utility bills to be invested in sustainable energy development for the poor. Sustainability Assessments to Value the Ecosphere (SAVE) can be administered by the UN.

Fourth, is the establishment of global organization, Global Initiative for Climate Cooling (GICC), to focus on developing and implementing mechanisms and market rules to facilitate sustainable investments in energy and related high pollution areas.

Tools. Investment. Determination. An ecological future.

In conclusion, we face a fundamental choice between building a sustainable ecological civilization or continue on the path to self-destruction. The time to choose is now. It's time to stand up to preserve our heritage and protect our futures.

Thank you.

Details of my remarks are further elucidated in my paper.

The Path Sutra

Sustainability is the path toward the transcendent One.

⊡

Sustainability is a reflection of and proof for the existence of a fundamental ethics and ethical principles.

⊡

Sustainability acting in creative response to all influences is an ever-evolving practice, more process and principle based than rule based.

⊡

This is the story of the Rabbi, a Hasidic master, on route to Shul on Yom Kippur, the holiest day, stopping and aiding a horse in grave distress and arriving late in a conscious manifestation of the prayer book calling for not a fast of sackcloth and ashes, but, in the words of Isaiah the prophet, of feeding the hungry, clothing the naked, and pursuing justice.

⊡

It was Darwin who understood the evolutionary benefits of human ethical and cooperative behavior. It was Kropotkin who saw cooperation as a generalized behavior broadly practiced for mutual survival.[74]

⊡

The frightened bird carried in the house by the cat allowed us to open the window to free her. The wasps inside let me catch them in the cup and release them outside many hundred of times without a buzz or a sting. The huge toad afloat in the middle of the lake climbed up my kayak paddle and walked up my arm to safety until we returned to shore. I watch the bees and wasps pollinate flowers. The second insect to arrive at a flower with a bee or wasp would consistently fly away as soon as it became aware of the bee or wasp already carrying pollen.

15

A BEE and a BIG

Sustainability is an expression of the health and potential for recovery of the ecosphere , as such it is a guide for our human well-being and prosperity.

How do we get from here to there, from an afflicted present to a sustainable future? What are the social mechanisms that can facilitate this transformation? Are their social mechanisms available that can help us pursue ecological sanity, sustainable economic growth, and social justice?

Can we really pursue, at the same time, solutions for climate change, sustainable economic growth, and social justice? Really?

Really. The following broad outlines of a grand bargain and strategy for an improved ecological future are clear:

- A global growth strategy builds efficient renewable energy and production infrastructure through global investments in sustainable economic growth;

- Advanced industrialized nations of the rich greatly reduce carbon dioxide emissions, pollution, depletion, and ecological damage;

- Industrializing nations of the poor move directly into balanced eco-systems and skip the high pollution, high ecological damage industrial past with aid in investment, knowledge, and technology from the rich to eliminate both pollution and poverty with the aim of justice and fairness for all.

We will consider a Basic Energy Entitlement (A BEE) and a Basic Income Guarantee (BIG) as two tools that help support global justice and global investment in efficient sustainable energy and sustainable economic growth. These tools are to be combined with the other elements of ecological transformation such as new market rules, ecological assessments that makes the price system send clear signals for sustainability, and definitions of fiduciary responsibility for corporations and government to conduct a monetary investment policy for ecological ends.

On the one hand, an ecological future is perfection of markets through elimination of externalities, and on the other hand it's the creation of economic, regulatory and legal structures that guide and condition the expression of markets to seek profit through sustainable means.

On the one hand, an ecological path is the building and optimization of global capital markets to finance and build the energy and productive infrastructure of an ecological future with many trillions of dollars.

On the other hand, the investments and enormous cash flows generated need be conditioned by the pursuit of justice and fairness manifested, for example, by the two mechanisms, of the Basic Energy Entitlement (BEE) and a Basic Income Guarantee (BIG).

The use of a Basic Energy Entitlement (BEE) will transfer funds from rich to poor to help finance renewable energy development. A Basic Income Guarantee (BIG), provides a basic level of income support for everyone to help lift people from poverty, and encourage further productive work. The BIG and the BEE together can be the global basis of a just and peaceful society for all while helping support and catalyze global investment in efficient renewable energy and ecological global growth strategy. Income from BEE investments can help fund the BIG.

CONVERGENCE OF BIOLOGICAL
AND SOCIAL EVOLUTION SUTRA

Sustainability is now the interaction of biological and social evolution.[75]

◌

Sustainability is both means and end.

◌

Sustainability is process and product.

◌

Sustainability is the practice of a moral ecology, the awareness that our actions have consequences, to the biosphere as well as to one another

◌

Sustainability is dynamic, not static; it inherently involves change and growth, but growth conditioned by limits, by growth resulting in ecological improvement, not ecological destruction.

◌

Sustainability refers to a trajectory that's neither vector nor circle, that by its nature never repeats and never ends as long as the ecosphere survives.

◌

Sustainability encompasses biological, mineral, and geophysical evolution. As humble a creature as algae helped change the nature of atmosphere and climate.

The history of sustainability is the history of life in motion, life shaping the ecosphere and the ecosphere shaping life.

Sustainability is an expression of the health and potential for recovery of the ecosphere; as such it is a guide for our human well-being and prosperity.

Sustainability is an attribute of the evolution of human society and ecosphere, always in motion, responsive to the dynamic interaction between the one and the many, between the members and constituents of the ecosphere and the changing system-state. This interaction, an exchange of information and of feedback of consequence, is cybernetic and therefore capable of being brought to self-consciousness and choice.

16

A BEE

Sustainability as applied economic practice is a recipe
for global growth and sustainable investment to slash
pollution, depletion, and ecological damage

A Basic Energy Entitlement (BEE) is designed to help address fundamental global problems:

- The rich and the rapidly industrializing produce far too much carbon dioxide from fossil fuels with associated ecological damage

- The rich and those rapidly industrializing need to dramatically reduce fossil fuel use and follow the efficient renewable energy path through investment in renewables

- The poor lack the capital and technology to follow a low-carbon efficient renewable energy path and are forced to follow a path of high-carbon dioxide, high-pollution, and high ecological damage

- There is no systematic global means to transfer capital and technology from rich to poor to help facilitate an ecologic global growth agenda that will benefit both rich and poor

What's a BEE?

A Basic Energy Entitlement (BEE) represents a global standard for ecological sustainability and a means of funding for making sustainable energy development possible for all. The more renewable the energy is, the less carbon and ecological damage will occur. The more efficient the system, the more useful the work output from less energy input. Physics can be on the side of a sustainable ecological global growth and investment plan catalyzed by a BEE.

A Basic Energy Entitlement (BEE) is based on a per capita annual entitlement, or lifeline, of 70 gigajoules of primary energy (19,443 kWh equivalents) and 3 tons of carbon dioxide emissions.[76]

Under a BEE all energy use would pay a uniform small charge, for example 7 tenths of a cent per kWh equivalent used for a United States BEE. The BEE would be administered on a fee-bate system. Energy use per person up to the 19,443 kWh per year per personal lifeline would be rebated to the consumer. Larger amounts would be used to fund BEE investments in efficient renewable technology

The BEE in Operation

A global plan for a Basic Energy Entitlement (BEE) uses assessments phased in for all energy use, on a kWh equivalent basis. The BEE simply converts all energy use to its heat value in BTUs (or British Thermal Units) to give an accurate measure of total energy use. To the BTU total is added the carbon dioxide associated with that energy.

The BEE assessment would be directly related to total energy use. Large industrial and commercial users would pay much larger BEE assessments. Competition would encourage cost cutting and energy efficiency. Individuals would be charged, for example, 1 cent per kWh equivalent if they exceeded their BEE lifeline.

What does 19,773 kWH of primary energy mean? A kilowatt-hour is equal to 3,414 BTU of heat. Each BTU is roughly equal to the heat released by burning a wooden kitchen match end to end. A kilowatt-hour is equal to burning a pile of 3,414 matches. This is quite a little bonfire.

The BEE Is a Tool for Ecological Transformation

The BEE can help to accomplish the following:

- Catalyze a global efficient renewable energy transformation, not simply as a revenue raising, or price signaling measure

- Build efficient renewables globally to replace fossil and nuclear energy

- Break as quickly as possible the business as usual connection between increasing energy use and increasing carbon dioxide

- Make processes much more efficient and by generating energy with zero carbon at point of production; and eventually with almost zero carbon in a world powered by efficient renewable energy for all processes

- Move the developing world directly to renewables and avoid the recapitulation of ecologically catastrophic large-scale fossil development

- Work with a Basic Income Guarantee (a BIG)as an important tool for both sustainable development and ecological justice

- Provide income from BEE investments that can be an ongoing source of income to help fund a BIG

The BEE is a means for transferring capital from high-energy users to low-energy users, and from rich to poor, both between and within nations. BEE assessments are levied at point of consumption on all energy use in terms of kilowatt-hour equivalent. The BEE is a fair means to help fund a global renewable energy transformation, and a tool for moving global per capita carbon emissions to a sustainable global level of three tons of carbon per person per year.

The BEE is a means to both encourage an efficient renewable energy transformation and to clearly account for an individual's and a nation's progress toward sustainability.

The BEE would work using personal accounts by social security numbers, for example, or by a unique BEE number. All energy purchases would be charged at the BEE rate at point of purchase, for example, seven tenths of a cent (.007 cent) per kWh equivalent and the information entered into your personal BEE account for energy purchases and associated carbon dioxide. Operating as an energy charge card, BEE fees could be added when the individual or family annual lifeline level is passed. The BEE system could also easily provide credits for smaller and low-income energy users on a monthly or yearly basis.

The BIG and BEE would more than rebate BEE payments made by the poor in both rich and poor nations. A BEE is a proposal to help catalyze the building of a global ecological civilization, one that can proceed within the context of grassroots economics, self-management, cooperative development, and market activity. The Solar Lights Project discussed in chapter 20 is a good example of grassroots efforts to what can made to reach out much more widely.

BEE investments internationally and domestically can help to fund efficient renewable investment and a sustainable future for the poor and for all people. Income from these productive investments can be used as a source to help fund a BIG.

The BEE and Global Energy Use and Carbon Dioxide Per Person

If global investment costs for climate change prevention are estimated at one percent of the global product of $74 trillion a year, or $740 billion, the primary burden would fall on the already industrialized world to help facilitate global ecological transition through global investment and technology transfer.

All nations should implement a BEE. The poorer and developing nations will use the BEE revenue internally. The 34 industrialized nations of the OECD account for over 47 trillion in GDP, about 64 percent of global total, and serve as be the primary source dedicated for international investment. All nations would have a BEE to for efficient renewable investment set at 1 percent of GDP.[77]

Nations like China with large economies, as well as huge populations still in poverty, that have enormous ecological challenges can invest their BEE domestically to reduce emissions and be supplemented by international BEE support to get the job of transformation accomplished.

Income over the long run from productive BEE investment would be used to help fund a BIG for the investing nations. Thus international partners in investment in an efficient renewable energy system in China would receive their portion of net project income to help fund a BIG at home, while Chinese BEE investment income would help fund China's BIG.

The United States share, based on 1 percent of $17.4 trillion GDP, would be $174 billion a year from 314 million Americans.

BEE assessments based on 86, 203 kWh equivalent use per person per year would be less than a penny a kilowatt hour or .007 cents/ kWh. The BEE, as noted, would operate partially as a fee-bate system. Annual BEE charges for the sustainable global lifeline entitlement of 19,773 kWh per person per year would be returned and credited back to individuals. The actual average United States BEE rate per person after the lifeline fee-bate would be $.006 per kWh equivalent.

What does this mean? The average American, based on 2012 data, using 86,203 kWh equivalents a year would pay $603 in a year, and receive a yearly fee-bate credit of $86 for a net annual BEE payment of $517. This $517 would be part of $167 billion dollar a year global investments in efficient renewables. The income from these investments would be used to help fund a United States BIG.

Assuming the investments start earning a modest 6 percent return in year three or $10 billion a year. Income would increase by $10 billion a year as investment proceeds. Over twenty years, $3.3 trillion would have been invested and $1.7 trillion returned as income to be used for the BIG, with the rate of BIG income reaching $189 billion a year by year 2020. This would pay in year 2020 the amount of $564 per person for a BIG person, or $2257 for a family of four.

Remember, renewables have zero fuel costs and modest operation and maintenance expense and would replace expensive and polluting fossil fuel expenses at the same time they power revitalized non-polluting economies, improve health and living standards, and create jobs and businesses.

The average American would pay net BEE assessments, above the lifeline as would the average Chinese at a much lower amount as shown by the following numbers:

- Global per capita energy use was 22,127 kWh equivalent in 2012.

- US per capita energy use in 2012 was equal to 86,203 kWh equivalent and 17.6 tons carbon per person per year. This means that US average energy use was 66,420 kWh equivalents greater then the BEE lifeline. For 319 million Americans this is $167 billion per year based on a 1 percent of GDP used for global programs for efficient renewable development for the poor.[78]

- China per capita total energy use in 2012 was 23,240 kWh and 6.2 tons carbon equivalent.

Regional energy use data from 1990–2008 reflects the dynamic of the industrialized rich world becoming relatively more efficient and emitting less from its past very high levels and the industrializing poor world emitting more from its past lower levels.

The BEE Is a Global Tool for Upending Business and Pollution as Usual

What's crucial to understand, is that the BEE personal per capita annual energy allowance (19,773 kWh equivalent and 3 tons carbon) was based by the United Nation Department of Economic and Social Affairs (UNSESA) on business as usual.

Business as usual still means a connection between energy use of all kinds and, overwhelmingly, fossil fuels and carbon dioxide production. A global energy system using efficient renewables would produce a dramatically lower amount of carbon dioxide as well as using this energy more efficiently and with much less ecological damage.

The BEE is meant to help break this connection between energy use and carbon pollution. It is a manifestation of the ecological turn that breaks the connection between economic growth and profit and ecological destruction. The BEE is a way of helping make economic growth mean ecological improvement and the regeneration of natural capital as well as the growth of finance capital.

To accomplish these steps is not the dis-establishment of markets or capitalism or the practice of economic contraction and the imposition of stringencies. It's much more about understanding the real world of renewable energy and the efficiencies made possible by the second law of thermodynamics. The profit-seeking behavior of markets, if given the proper market rules, economic signals and incentives will be applied for sustainable ends.

Efficiency Matters and Net Carbon

The BEE is an incitement to change, both in terms of replacing fossil fuels with renewables and in increasing efficiency of existing processes. Efficient renewables are double winners. They replace fossil fuels with zero pollution sun, wind, water, and use that energy much more efficiently.[79]

According to the EIA an average coal plant burning hard coal, for example, burned 10,089 BTUs and released 2.07 pounds of carbon dioxide to produce one kilowatt hour of electricity with an energy value of 3,414 kWh (33.8 percent efficiency in terms of the relationship between coal energy in and electric energy out).

If that electricity was produced by renewables with zero fossil fuels using wind, sun, water, or geothermal it would consume zero carbon in generation.

Efficiency matters, but the direct consequences in terms of carbon dioxide is of much less significance in terms of renewables. The top efficiency of commercial solar cells is now around 20 percent (and rising) converting sunlight to power; wind is around 45-50 percent.

Efficiency matters, your gasoline driven car is likely to be only around 20 percent (or less) efficient in converting gasoline fuel to motion while spewing carbon dioxide. Your electric car likely to be three times or more efficient, around 60 percent, in converting stored energy to motion releasing zero carbon per mile driven in a renewably powered electric grid. This means this electric vehicle has about 1/3 of net carbon of a gasoline engine even if the electricity still came from coal or natural gas as a transitional step.[80]

And, remember that a streamlined and light, electric vehicle fleet will use far less energy per mile then traditional gas guzzlers, further reducing net carbon even from a grid that still had some fossil fuel power plants.

BEE Assessments of OECD Nations

Here is total national BEE contribution in dollars based on 1 percent of GDP and per capita average BEE payment in dollars for the advanced industrial nation of the OECD. This represents an international investment pool for efficient renewable development and source of funds to help fund a BIG. The national BEE rate per kWh equivalent will depend on average kWH equivalent use. The BEE assessment would be recalculated every year based on GDP and population changes and total energy use in kilowatt-hour equivalents. Table below has latest OECD data for 2014.

BEE Calculations[81]

OECD Nation	2014 GDP in Billion $	1% GPD in Billion $	Population Millions (2012)	Average BEE Per $ Capita
Australia	1,063	10.63	22.72	$468
Austria	394	3.94	8.43	$467
Belgium	479	4.79	11.13	$430
Canada	1,566	15.66	34.89	$449
Chile	397	3.97	17.4	$228
Czech Republic	320	3.2	10.51	$304
Denmark	253	2.53	5.59	$453
Estonia	35	0.35	1.33	$263
Finland	218	2.18	5.41	$403
France	2,572	25.72	63.51	$405
Germany	3,690	36.9	81.93	$450
Greece	286	2.86	11.09	$258
Hungary	241	2.41	9.92	$243
Iceland	14	0.14	0.32	$438
Ireland	221	2.21	4.59	$481
Israel	271	2.71	7.91	$343
Italy	2,132	21.32	60.92	$350
Japan	4,636	46.36	127.52	$364
Korea	1,732	17.32	.50	$346
Luxembourg	55	0.55	0.53	$1,038
Mexico	2,120	21.2	117.05	$181
Netherlands	803	8.03	16.75	$479

(continued)

OECD Nation	2014 GDP in Billion $	1% GPD in Billion $	Population Millions (2012)	Average BEE Per $ Capita
New Zealand	165	1.65	4.42	$373
Norway	333	3.33	5.02	$663
Poland	943	9.43	38.53	$245
Portugal	295	2.95	10.51	$281
Slovak Republic	149	1.49	5.4	$276
Slovenia	62	0.62	2.06	$301
Spain	1,567	15.67	46.15	$340
Sweden	437	4.37	9.52	$459
Switzerland	473	4.73	7.91	$598
Turkey	1,460	14.6	75.17	$194
United Kingdom	2,530	25.3	63.7	$397
United States	17,419	174.19	313.87	$555
Euro area	**13,040**	**130**	**332**	$392
OECD–Total	**49,332**	**493**	**1,245**	
World			**7,080**	

BEE Calculations (*continued*)

National Accounts at a Glance

A BEE in New England

Let's consider what a Basic Energy Entitlement (a BEE) means for a typically frugal New Englander.

The woman is using modest amounts of electricity, driving a 30 mpg car, and keeping her home thermostat down at 65 degrees. Although frugal by US standards, this means she uses annually 72,700 kWh equivalent for electricity, driving, and heating. This would exceed the BEE lifeline of 19,773 kWh by 52,527 kWh.

Does this mean, to meet BEE requirements she would upend her life by biking to work instead of driving, taking cold showers rather than hot showers, having the thermostat at 55 degrees in winter, and using candles instead of electric light? No it does not. In fact, the changes for meeting the BEE carbon requirements would improve her life by slashing her driving costs with an electric vehicle, dramatically cutting heating and hot water costs with an air-to-air heat pump, and trimming her lighting costs with LEDs.

What's needed is not stringency, but use of investment capital that can be paid for from savings through her monthly utility bills. That's what the BEE is about—the basis for a creative mechanism to help lift all of us toward a sustainable and fair future.

At .007 per kilowatt hour assessed at the pump on her electricity and heat bills, she would pay a net annual BEE assessment, after lifeline fee-bate, in 2015 of $370 a year, about 7 dollars a week for direct energy use for her yearly kWh-use above the BEE lifeline. She'd also be charged indirectly for the BEE paid for energy used in industrial and food production, airplanes, mass transit, trucking, water and sewer, and everything else.

A New Englander's BEE Details: 2015

Electricity

How does this personal use break down? Today, our New Englander uses 500 kilowatt hours per month, 6,000 kWh a year for electricity in her home for lights, computers, television, microwave, and everything else plugged into the electric system. This amounts to about 30 percent of total in terms of energy for the BEE.

But if this electricity was fossil fuel grid power, which has an average input value of 11,600 BTU per kWh, or about 29 percent efficiency from power plant to home, then she has already taken up her entire BEE total without transportation and without any fuel consumption for heating.

Renewable electricity, it is important to remember, not only avoids pollution from fossil fuel combustion, but can also be more efficient in second law terms. It pays double dividends of less carbon and more work out for less energy in. A heat pump, for example, taking advantage of the Carnot cycle, can easily get three times more useful energy out than the amount of electricity consumed, compared to a less then 10 percent second law efficiency of conventional oil fossil fuel combustion in contrast to 85-90 percent first-law efficiency. In the second law of thermodynamics terms, most of the capacity to do work of oil or natural gas is wasted through combustion to heat air.

An efficient renewable energy transformation will mean a greatly expanded use of electricity to power our vehicles, light, heat and cool our homes, and power our factories. This is central to a sustainable global energy convergence.

Driving

Gasoline has 114,000 BTUs per gallon. Drive 10,000 miles a year in a car that gets 30 miles per gallon and you use 333 gallons that's equal to 11,130 kWh. The BEE at .007/kWh equivalent would mean a payment of 23 cents a gallon at the pump. About $.03 per gallon would be a lifeline fee-bate refund, for a net annual BEE assessment payment of 20 cents a gallon.

This 30 mpg gasoline car driven 10,000 miles releases 3.33 tons of CO-2 per year (about 20 pounds per gallon of gas), already exhausting a per capita CO2 annual carbon dioxide allowance. It will have also consumed the equivalent of 11,130 kWh of primary energy.

An electric vehicle, available today, at 3kWh per mile (with much higher efficiencies demonstrated), would use 3,333 kWh of primary energy from a renewably powered grid for 10,000 miles and release zero carbon directly. Net carbon would depend on nature of material manufacture. Again, this would be small in a non-fossil fuel energy system.

The mechanical transformation of internal combustion is very inefficient, as well as polluting. Only 17–21 percent of gasoline energy is transferred to wheels with much productive energy lost to friction, exhaust, heat. In sharp contrast, for electric cars, 59-62 percent of energy from the gird is transferred to wheels (DOE, 2015). If your car was electric, even if the generation was not renewable, you would have about a 3x higher 2nd law efficiency and a much lower net BEE assessment.

Heating

If she burns 1,000 gallon of fuel oil to heat her home, that's another 41,007 kWh equivalents or 56 percent of her total.

A gallon of fuel oil has 140,000 BTUs, and if operating at 85 percent first law conversion efficiency it delivers 119,00 BTUs of heat and releases 23.4 pounds of carbon dioxide.

BEE assessments would be 28 cents a gallon of fuel oil, and she'd receive about a 4 cent a gallon lifeline fee-bate refund. Her total net payment for 1,000 gallons of No.2 oil would be $240 a year.

Say she switches instead to a new air-to-air heat pump system, available today, to provide heat and cooling. The heat pump produces more energy out, the heat taken from the air, and then energy in. If the heat pump has a modest coefficient of performance (C.O.P.) of 3.0 then for every BTU in 3,414 to run the compressors fans and pumps, the device delivers 10,242 BTUs of heat out. Note that C.O.P.s of five or six will be delivered as manufacturing experience gets a bit closer to theoretical possibilities.

BEE assessment for the heating equivalent of 1,000 gallons of oil delivered by the heat pump would be based on 13, 669 kWh consumed or $96 a year before lifeline fee-bate of $13 for a net annual total of $83 compared to $240 BEE for oil. And, of course, if the electricity was provided by renewables there would be zero direct carbon, compared to 23,400 pounds of carbon dioxide from burning oil.

If the electricity running the heat pumps was coal fired, releasing 2.07 pounds per kWh, total carbon for 13,669 kWh to power the heat pump would be 28,294 pounds produced at the power plant and therefore no carbon savings compared to oil.

If she uses the electric heat pump instead, and she's buying electricity generated from natural gas, she'll release 14,040 pounds of carbon, a 42 percent reduction, assuming that methane emissions from gas drilling and fracking were properly controlled.

The BEE in New England During Efficient Renewable Transition: 2025

Our typical frugal New Englander now drives an electric vehicle that's plugged in overnight to charge. She heats and cools here home with air-to-air heat pump. She's changed to LED lights, added more insulation and better controls and has improved her overall energy efficiency 25 percent. At the same time, she's increased her electric use for her electric car and her heat pump and now uses 1,300 kWh per month or 15,600 kWh per year.

Guess what. Her net annual Bee assessment is zero. In fact, as a small user below the BEE lifeline she may be eligible for grants to improve her renewables and her efficiency.

Assume that the grid is now 50 percent renewables. Her carbon for her electricity use of 15,600 kWh per year, assuming natural gas generation, is now down to 4.5 tons per year. That's down to what is now the global average. At 75 percent renewables she would be at a sustainable 3 tons carbon per year rate.

This is the possible future of a global ecological growth strategy that boosts efficiency and slashes carbon and makes economic growth mean ecological improvement.

When people like Elon Musk say a 100 percent renewable future is ours for the making, we should listen and move ahead as global leaders seizing the day and profit stream. Now!

Future of the BEE

The next step for the BEE that I will undertake is to develop plans for sustainable investments and technology transfers. BEE fund transfers should avoid the provision of funds to government. They should instead focus on direct investment partnership, include capitalizing Grameen Bank types and other self-help groups, capitalize resolving funds to provide low or zero interest renewable development loans, and fund educational institutions for mass training in decentralized renewable development.

There were 1.3 billion people as of 2014 without access to electricity and 2.7 billion who use traditional biomass for cooking with its attendant indoor air pollution. To achieve the UN goals of a Decade of Sustainable Energy for All requires a robust funding means to facilitate a renewable energy transformation and avoid the choice of the pursuit of a fossil fuel path. The BEE is such a global instrument.[82]

I am helping, for example, a grassroots project, Solar Lights, working with students in South Africa to assemble and sell small PV systems for lighting and cell phone charging to replace expensive candles, kerosene, and battery purchases.[83] Solar Lights will be discussed in greater detail in chapter 20.

A BEE is an example of a way to be able to both provide support for proven plans needing capital and technical support and to help seed multiple efforts and then scale up, allowing successful entrepreneurial pilot projects to become new models and part of a broad transformative effort.

Economic Growth As
Ecological Improvement Sutra[84]

The challenge, at bottom, for such a sustainable high economic growth and low pollution order is political, not technical.

◻

Replace the world's high pollution fossil and nuclear energy systems with efficient renewable resources will be a prime example of economic growth leading to ecological improvement in the context of creation of sustainable jobs, sustainable businesses, sustainable communities.

◻

Sustainability as applied economic practice is a recipe for global growth and sustainable investment to slash pollution, depletion, and ecological damage.

◻

The business song of sustainability means increased quarterly earnings per share or EPS.

◻

The polluter and poisoners, by and large, cannot and will not be counted upon to help themselves and save us. They will cling like grim death, ours and theirs, to their poison profits from the trillions of dollars of value imputed to fossil fuels in the ground to be burned with the poison pouring unmitigated into the atmosphere.

◻

We do not need to reply upon the good will of polluters. Rather we have in our hands the ability to act, to adopt by political action new market rules that will forbid some practices and embrace others, and to make through ecological assessments levying of fees and taxes for what is sustainable less expensive, with ability to gain market share and become more profitable, and what is polluting the environment more expensive to lose market share and become less profitable.

▣

Political action is likely to mean more than letters to Congress. It means acts like the Sioux their erecting teepees on the route across their land of the Keystone Pipeline and forging an Indian-Cowboy Alliance that so far has prevailed in South Dakota.

▣

Political action may mean not just thousands or tens of thousands in the streets, but millions demanding healing change before the consequences of pollution foreclose our opportunities.

▣

Sustainability can oppose what cannot continue with what can, with humanity as mediator.

17

A BIG

From the village to continental groups of nations, the question of sustainability rising will confront issues of business and pollution and short-term profit as usual or long term benefit, and indeed the issue of self-destruction or a prosperous future.

History and Spirit of a BIG

The idea of a Basic Income Guarantee has roots across the political spectrum. It's based on the broadly held understanding that people come into the world and into adulthood typically with widely differing opportunities and advantages based on the past and historical circumstance.

In the pamphlet "Agrarian Justice," that Tom Paine wrote in 1795–6, he said:

> Poverty . . . is a thing created by that which is called civilized life. It exists not in the natural state. . . . But the fact is that the condition of millions, in every country in Europe, is far worse than if they had been born before civilization began . . . Cultivation is at least one of the greatest natural improvements ever made by human invention. . . . But the landed monopoly that began with it has produced the greatest evil. It has dispossessed more than half the inhabitants of every nation of their natural inheritance, without providing for them, as ought to have been done, an indemnification for that loss, and has thereby created a species of poverty and wretchedness that did not exist before . . . I . . . propose . . . To create a national fund,

out of which there shall be paid to every person, when arrived at the age of twenty-one years, the sum of fifteen pounds sterling, as a compensation in part, for the loss of his or her natural inheritance, by the introduction of the system of landed property: And also, the sum of ten pounds per annum, during life, to every person now living, of the age of fifty years, and to all others as they shall arrive at that age.

On Right and Left the concept of providing every citizen with a cash award of some sort to overcome historical injustice and market failure, past and present, and provide an opportunity for independence and self-management has been embraced by the broadest spectrum of thinkers, economists, and politicians. It was supported on the Right by F. A. Hayek and Milton Friedman, and Richard Nixon and on the Left by Bertram Russell, Andre Gorz,[85] and Lyndon Johnson.

The concept has attracted a diverse range of economists, philosophers, politicians, and moralists of all stripes to attempt to directly remedy injustice and unfair circumstance in the form of government cash grant. Even the most resolute market mavens, fearful of planning and government power, found a BIG, in some form, a necessary response to the apparently inescapable problems of market failure and contingency.

The chains of injustice and evil are cut in a *deus ex machina* fashion by a cash grant with no or few strings that frees people from dire poverty and from the sometimes unwanted, unwarranted, and costly ministrations of the bureaucratic state. The poor may or may not need other assistance. But what they definitively need is cash that will facilitate getting on with their lives.

I want to make clear that building a prosperous ecological future need not carry banner of right or left, but take advantage of concepts all along the political spectrum. The BIG and the BEE are examples of such ideologically hybrid mechanisms that can help us move ahead.

Basic Income Guarantee (BIG)

The general adoption of a Basic Income Guarantee (BIG) for all will provide sufficient income to meet most basic needs. The BIG is both a replacement for welfare and incentive for work to earn income beyond the basic level.

The Basic Income Guarantee (BIG) is a government guarantee that no one's income shall fall below a level necessary to meet most basic needs. A BIG is an invitation to work further for more income, and a replacement for existing welfare programs and their bureaucracies.[86]

In Alaska, for example, since 1982 the Alaska Permanent Fund, financed by revenues from oil and gas and other mineral production, pays a varying yearly dividend, to all residents of living in Alaska for one year or more. This was $1,884 per person in 2014.[87]

Brazil's Bolsa Familia pays 70 reais person per month (about $35)for families below the poverty line of 140 reais. Operating for over 10 years the Bolsa Família reaches 45 million people in 11 million families, a major portion of the poor. The Bolsa Família has both helped families move out of grinding poverty and supporting the education of their children.

Annual Dividends from Oil and Gas Revenues Paid to All Alaskan Residents Living in Alaska for One Year or More			
2001	$1,850.00	2008	$2,069.00
2002	$1,540.00	2009	$1,305.00
2003	$1,107.00	2010	$1,081.00
2004	$919.84	2011	$1,174.00
2005	$845.76	2012	$878.00
2006	$1,106.96	2013	$900.00
2007	$1,654.00	2014	$1,884.00

Dinalva Pereira de Moura, whose family lives in the Varjão favela in the Federal District, says the Bolsa Família "has been a marvelous thing for me and my family. I have three children and my husband is unemployed. The Bolsa Família helps me buy food. Sometimes I can even buy fruit for the children. My children know that when we receive the money, they will have more to eat, and that makes them happier. And they don't skip school, because they know that the money depends on their going."[88]

A BIG may be understood as an expanded and generalized version of social security and Medicare that has been enormously successful in alleviating poverty and destitution of seniors.

A BIG with its ideological multi-denominational support offers a number of important advantages in helping to facilitate a global ecological transformation. First, in even modest amounts, like Brazil's Bolsa Família, it has proven in various places to be very helpful both in relieving impoverishment and stimulating further activity through the ministration simply of cash without government supervision. The BIG is simply a commitment of a percentage of social capital to permit all to enjoy a basic income. A BIG can be conditioned to favor the use and purchase of sustainable products. Thus, a BIG debit card can reward purchasing of sustainably rated products, providing another market incentive for sustainability.

Second, the BIG, in a future with ever-increasing technological employment, is a necessary measure where useful and non-ecologically destructive work will be increasingly hard to find. In this fashion, a BIG is a means for limitation of hyper-consumption and production, and at the same time a support for a base level of income and spending.

As a social justice principle, the BIG is the fulfillment of a universal commitment for the end of desperate poverty, a step necessary for both the alleviation of misery and for the regeneration of natural capital. Ecological choices cannot be forced upon those struggling to feed themselves. People without access to clean water, clean air, housing, medicine, and education become easy marks for exploitation of their land and themselves. Their desperate lives call forth desperate measures for survival.

A Basic Income Guarantee (BIG) and a Basic Energy Entitlement (BEE) are examples of two complementary global mechanisms for the global pursuit of both a renewable energy future upon a framework of fairness and social justice. An ecological civilization will not emerge simply by building green machines in a world riven by the intractable misery of billions. Income generated from BEE investments can help fund the BIG.

Sustainability and an ecological global growth agenda as a successful global practice is ultimately about the global success of an ecological justice movement that ends both poverty and ecological pillage. This is a recipe for a richer, more interdependent, and more just world.

The BEE and the BIG in Action

The integration of a BEE with a BIG helps creates a global dynamic of ecological justice. The BEE and the BIG are expressions of the global pursuit of sustainability and transition to a zero-waste zero pollution economy characteristic of a sustainable ecological civilization.

Economic growth can and must mean ecological improvement and the regeneration of natural capital as a consequence of the growth of finance capital. A BIG and a BEE are strong affirmative steps in this direction.

The transformation from business and pollution as usual to an "ecological civilization" is a not an impossible task, or too complex, or without specific ways to take meaningful steps forward accomplishing.

Successful pursuit of an ecological global growth agenda by business and government is the path forward to definitively demonstrate that markets and corporate capitalism and democracy can work for ecological ends, and that neither are irredeemably compromised, and that we must start over with some new and yet to be defined social order.

The central message of *Sustainability Sutra* is that we can and must embark upon a program of change that will help transform the global capitalist market system to follow the path of sustainable economic growth that means the regeneration of natural capital and ecological justice for all. But in our pursuit of sustainable and profitable ends we need to rip nothing out by the roots and start over.

What I am describing is a series of transformative reforms that have no automatic identification with right or left. These reforms embrace markets as a key global means for ecological transformation through the pursuit of an ecological growth agenda. At the same time, it uses new market rules, ecological assessments, and regulations, to make the price system send clear signals for sustainability. It redefines fiduciary responsibility to be a matter of following the laws for business and government to establish sustainable conduct and support for social justice.

Systematically and comprehensively making the cost of sustainable goods and services cheaper and their providers more profitable, with larger market shares and higher quarterly earnings per share as well as other things, is also a plan for the regeneration of natural capital. While this is hardly friendly to current business and pollution as usual, ecological growth is based on the continued health, and indeed the healthy growth, of the market system.

By closing the door on both externalities that lead to pollution, depletion, and ecological damage combined with the pursuit of social justice under an ecological market system, "all that is solid" no longer "melts into air," as Marx described the operation of capitalism in the 19th century.[89] Using the price system as a tool to help eliminate externalities is, in effect, a 21st century radical reform that chooses markets and market forces over pollution and ecological degradation and chooses a path toward building a sustainable ecological civilization.

SUSTAINABILITY RISING SUTRA[90]

Sustainability is a ubiquitous expression of life.

◘

The pace and development of sustainability rising as social practice is the expression of an emergent phenomenon whose nature will both be unpredictable and open new pathways.

◘

As a global movement, sustainability is likely to be a convergence of actions from below and from above. Sustainability will arise from individuals making choices and taking actions and from nations and continental groups of nations consciously pursuing sustainability and economic growth that leads to ecological improvement.

◘

Villages and neighborhoods anywhere in the world can lead and provide singular examples that can become the model for the enthusiastic practice of smaller nations like Denmark for following sustainable pathways.

◘

Sustainability is a global matter. Ultimately our future will be decided by the actions of the large population centers and economic leaders, the current largest polluters decisively choosing to follow the sustainable pathway and pursue global economic growth and ecological improvement. Global carbon pollution from fossil fuel use is still rising and economic growth in the aggregate still leads to pollution, depletion, and eco-logical damage. The pursuit of short-term profit still often trumps well-being. But the sustainability ques-tion is being raised around the world. This is contested terrain—the crucial social, political and economic question for the 21st century.

⊡

The sustainability question has been strangely deformed in the United States into a political issue where the Republican Party has become the party of climate change deniers and mega-polluters. The Republicans were historically the leaders in environ-mental protection, from T.R. Roosevelt to Richard Nixon, as the party representing the owners of prop-erty with a self-interest in stewardship, embracing both economic expansion and countervailing limita-tion as a smart growth party. The embrace of an eco-logical global growth agenda is likely to be the future of a revitalized American conservatism in the 21st cen-tury if conservatism is to remain politically relevant.

⊡

Globally, what is in dispute is the method to achieve sustainability. In Britain the ruling conservative party pursues a green agenda to meet, for example, climate change goals. In India the new right-wing govern-ment is aggressively pursuing mass solar development.

⊡

China, global leader in photovoltaic production, solar hot water, and split system heat pumps, has embraced building an ecological civilization as a matter of state policy at the same time when coal plants and cars make air toxic in major cities and carbon pollution increases.

◻

China, under technologically sophisticated leadership, has the ability to make the major choices controlling production, consumption, and investment decisions to pursue sustainable ends as well as adopting new market rules and ecological consumption taxation policies to send price signals for sustainability. China's taxation system already is more reliant on consumption taxes as opposed to income taxes, and therefore able to make their consumption tax regimes send effective ecological price signals.

◻

From the village to continental groups of nations, the question of sustainability rising will confront issues of business and pollution and short- term profit as usual, or long-term benefit, and indeed the issue of self-destruction or a prosperous future.

◻

Unfortunately, there is no reform-by-date posted for business and pollution as usual. There is no way to clearly understand the nature and pace of irreversible, emergent, and catastrophic change except in retrospect when, of course, it is too late. Prudence, common sense, and net economic benefit should make the pursuit of sustainability an immediate priority except for the most shortsighted polluters determined to continue to profit by their misdeeds. We can do better.

18

Be Afraid, Be Very Afraid

The human brain's average alpha frequency measured by encephalography is 7. 83 hertz. The earth's own pervasive natural electrical frequency is 7.83 hertz. This so-called Schumann resonance was theoretically predicted in 1952 by physicist Dr. Winfried Otto Schumann.

The current political discourse is about home-grown ISIS terrorists, and the need for all of us to be afraid, very afraid. This is complemented by the ever widening wars against terror and the active battlegrounds that have much to do with the control of oil and natural gas. We are regaled by US Navy commercials, a marketing trope for gathering recruits, no longer promoted as "a global force for good," but now showing dots on a globe map representing pervasive global network of bases "protecting all we hold dear at home."

This is what amounts to a lowest common denominator statement in support of protecting the *homeland*, and, by inference, a global network whose mission is maintaining our pleasures and privileges under business as usual. This is advertising and rhetoric, not command decisions.

The military, it should be acknowledged, are among those most concerned abut the catastrophic security problems unleashed by climate change and ecological collapse. President Obama now makes it clear that climate change is a national security issue. But there is still a disconnect between rhetoric, behavior, and deployments and between saying the right thing and consistently doing the right thing. Apparently it's still possible to approve Shell's plan to drilling the Arctic at the same time you are raising strategic concerns about climate change.

Obama's blunt remarks on May 20, 2015, to the graduates of the U.S. Coast Guard Academy, nevertheless, deserves attention:

> Climate change, and especially rising seas, is a threat to our homeland security, our economic infrastructure, the safety and health of the American people. Already, today, in Miami and Charleston, streets now flood at high tide. . . . It's estimated that a further increase in sea level of just one foot by the end of this century could cost our nation $200 billion.
>
> In New York Harbor, the sea level is already a foot higher than a century ago—which was one of the reasons Superstorm Sandy put so much of lower Manhattan underwater. During Sandy, the Coast Guard mounted a heroic response, along with our National Guard and Reserve. . . .
>
> Climate change poses a threat to the readiness of our forces. Many of our military installations are on the coast, including, of course, our Coast Guard stations. Around Norfolk, high tides and storms increasingly flood parts of our Navy base and an airbase. In Alaska, thawing permafrost is damaging military facilities. Out West, deeper droughts and longer wildfires could threaten training areas our troops depend on.
>
> So politicians who say they care about military readiness ought to care about this, as well. . . .
>
> Now, everything I've discussed with you so far is about preparing for the impacts of climate change. But we need to be honest—such preparation and adaptation alone will not be enough . . . the only way the world is going to prevent the worst effects of climate change is to slow down the warming of the planet.
>
> Some warming is now inevitable. But there comes a point when the worst effects will be irreversible. And time is running out. And we all know what needs to happen. It's no secret the world has to finally start reducing its carbon

emissions—now. And that's why I've committed the United States to leading the world on this challenge.[91]

It is the pursuit of global policies for ecological economic growth and for social justice that, in the long run, will protect us much more than military strength and the pursuit of narrow self-interest defined by the control of fossil fuels and strategic minerals. Global ecological prosperity and ecological justice is a hard-headed approach, based not on the short-term self-interest of corporate oligopolies, but in a shared vision of ecological growth and peace.

LIFE AND MIND
ARE COEXTENSIVE SUTRA[92]

Our view of humanity as an exceptional and privileged guest on Hotel Earth, provided with "resources" to be consumed and turned into our cash and our pleasure, surrounded by an unchanging landscape unconscious, mute, and isolated beings, is self-delusion.

◫

Communication, indeed mind, is a pervasive character of life. The trajectory of sustainability, in retrospect, is the creation of mind, from responsive behavior in even the simplest animals and plants recognized by Darwin, that manifests as self-consciousness.

◫

Life and mind are coextensive.

◫

Plants "talk" in their own fashion. Until recently most people have not tried to understand this.

◫

Dumb as a cabbage is likely an oxymoron. Life is communicative even in the vegetable kingdom. Bean plants when attacked by aphids will release volatile organic compounds into the air as chemicals signaling neighbors to release other chemicals to repel aphids and attract predatory wasps that feed on aphids. And if these plants are also linked at the roots by fungal mycelium, their fungal symbionts send warnings that make connected members repel aphids and attract wasps.

◘

Mind and communication and cybernetic feedback are fundamental to the history of life and sustainability.

◘

The human brain's average alpha frequency measured by encephalography is 7.83 hertz.

◘

The earth's own pervasive natural electrical frequency is 7.83 hertz. This so-called Schumann resonance was theoretically predicted in 1952 by physicist Dr. Winfried Otto Schumann. The Earth behaves like a giant battery on the basis of the electrical potential in the 60-mile-wide space between the ionosphere, positively charged by solar wind, and the earth's negatively charged surface.

◘

Sustainability and self-consciousness, if having no distinct and reductionist planetary limits, also should have no limits upon its course beyond that of physical law.

◘

The future course of sustainability and self-consciousness is moving rapidly toward the integration of mind and machine.

◘

Will self-consciousness produce the self-conscious and self-reproducing machine that becomes another part of sustainability and shaper of the system state and future direction?

⊡

Sustainability is Janus faced in many aspects. Its daily work is the maintenance of the steady state that includes the operation of chaotic dynamics that given proper conditions will lead swiftly to establishment of a new and dramatically altered equilibrium. Perhaps sustainability can and will take a further leap.

⊡

Will there be a convergence upon self-consciousness as intelligent mind as energy field freed from both biological and machine bodies and their hybrid forms as part of the evolution of sustainability?

⊡

Is this the natural law of universal self-consciousness, of the web of life, of the history of sustainability?

⊡

Is the natural course of things the transcendent vision that animated and inspired the cave paintings of our ancestors that leads us toward heights limited only by physical law and our imaginations?

⊡

Is Earth just a primitive backwater, still taking baby steps in a universe pervaded by intelligence and self-consciousness?

19

A Twenty-Eighth Amendment
to the Constitution

*Sustainability is the evolution of an industrial to
an ecological civilization.*

It's time for an ecological conduct amendment, a twenty-eighth amendment, to the United States Constitution. We must choose to follow either an ecological path and prosperity or continue along the road of business and pollution as usual leading to ecological self-destruction. It's time to make the pursuit of an ecological path part of our nation's guiding constitution.

What Lincoln once said about slavery is also true for pollution:

> "A house divided against itself cannot stand. I believe this government cannot endure, permanently half *slave* and half *free*. I do not expect the Union to be *dissolved*—I do not expect the house to *fall*—but I *do* expect it will cease to be divided. It will become *all* one thing or *all* the other."

> —ABRAHAM LINCOLN
> House Divided Speech,
> Springfield, Illinois, June 16, 1858[93]

We must become either an ecological or an industrial civilization. And since an industrial civilization is self-destructive and cannot endure, we have no other real choice not only for survival and prosperity than to follow the ecological path.

Perhaps this means for the United States in the 21st century, codifying for all time the determination, after a hard-won struggle, to continue following the ecological path, the passage of a twenty-eighth constitutional amendment for ecological rights and responsibilities, like the Thirteenth, Fourteenth, and Fifteenth Amendments following the Civil War for equal protection and due process under the law for all, ending slavery and guaranteeing all adult men the right to vote.

Amendment Twenty-Eight on Ecological Conduct

Section 1. The rights and responsibilities to protect, sustain and enjoy ecological well being and health shall be a fundamental principle of these United States.

Section 2. Economic growth in these United States shall be guided by principles under law that leads to the improvement and regeneration of natural capital and the advancement of social and ecological justice.

Section 3. Fiduciary responsibility under law shall be defined as the prudent management of finance capital, the improvement and regeneration of natural capital, and the advancement of social and ecological justice.

20

Solar Lights for South African Youth:

Educate, Train, and Employ South African Youth in Small Solar System Production Sales and Maintenance

Sustainability is thus a biological process with a social resonance and a social process with a biological resonance.

A global renewable transformation will not appear magically or be dropped down fully formed from above by Act of Congress, or by decisions by the United Nations, or by new product announcements and investments by global solar companies.

The singular moments that historically mark moments of transformation were the result of a long social, political, and economic struggle rising from the grassroots in response to injustice. For example, passage of the Civil Rights Act of 1964 and the Nineteenth Amendment to the Constitution ratified in 1920 on women's right to vote were the culmination of long struggles. Woodrow Wilson and Lyndon Johnson both played important roles as president in the final political solution, but Johnson did not "give" African Americans civil rights, nor did Wilson "give" women the right to vote. The Civil Rights Act and the Eighteenth Amendment were, at bottom, expressions of the victory of transformative social movements.

Similarly, a global renewable energy transformation to replace fossil fuels and nuclear energy will be an expression not simply of superior technological evolution, like the rise of coal to replace wood and water power and of oil to replace coal, but an expression of broad and insistent grassroots pressure of social movements to transform business and pollution as usual that is leading us all toward mutual self-destruction.

Yes, the technological issues will shape the nature of the facts on the ground, but the timely and, above all, global renewable transformation will be a response to ever rising grassroots pressure for change and transformation.

The Solar Lights Project of Ed Bender and Pamela Ulicny

The Solar Lights project is a good example of the development of such grassroots efforts, among many thousands of others, that will be the basis of not just demands for change but of education, empowerment, and building of a just and sustainable renewable future.

A global renewable energy transformation will be a combination of the following:

⦿ Technology and investment capital transfer

⦿ Empowerment and education

⦿ Entrepreneurial verve

⦿ Small initiatives becoming very large scale

⦿ The expression of social and ecological justice

⦿ The building and ongoing evolution of sustainable technical, economic, political, and social forms

The Solar Lights project is an example of small developing initiatives bringing together an interesting and unlikely combination of players. This is how an inventor and small businessman from New Hampshire and a teacher from Pennsylvania have sparked effort to bring solar lights and sustainable business to South African townships.

Ed Bender from Warner, New Hampshire

I met Ed in Warner when he owned a video store rented videos and sold candy to kids. Ed told me he built his business "one laughy-taffy at a time."

Ed is also a self-taught electronics and solar energy inventor. After he worked in video rentals, Ed started a company, Sundance Solar, a business selling a wide variety of solar gear on the Internet that included a number of devices Ed either fabricated or invented, including one of the first sophisticated backpack charging devices for cell phones and small electronics. It worked, but only at a price point, that at the time was too high.

Ed also designed a plan for Fiji of using solar arrays to recharge batteries for a small fee per charge for end users to build sustainable local enterprise. Users would no longer have to buy more expensive disposable batteries and polluting kerosene. The batteries would power solar lights and cell phones.

Today, Ed is developing and selling solar educational kits, the Sunbender line, currently with about 20 products for do-it-yourselfers and for teachers and educational-supply companies to train students in constructing small and inexpensive working solar devices like solar LED lights in a jar.[94]

The prewired, no-soldering, solar light kit retails for $22.95. The solar electricity learning kit sells for $49.95. The solar battery 50 mA charger kit for 2AAs retails for $13.95.

Pamela Ulicny, a biology and environmental science teacher at Tri-Valley Jr/Sr High School in Hegins, Pennsylvania

In 2011 Pam was selected by Toyota International Teacher Program and the Institute of International Education (IIE) as one of twenty-four teachers in the United States to visit South Africa.

"All I could think of is how wrong it felt to be sitting on a coach bus, looking down at the township and its folk, taking pictures of them as if they were some type of attraction, and then knowing that I was going to eat my fill in a quality restaurant and sleep in a four-star hotel that night."

Pam Ulicny realized that when students leave school they have no safe and consistent lighting in their homes to study. She began working with Mark Gamble of Educo, Africa, who was engaged with impoverished youth in South African townships and their families. Pam and Mark came up a plan of fusing science education with the needs of the people in South Africa by finding a low-cost way to provide solar-powered lanterns to people with no access to electricity.

Ulicny created a science education unit tied directly to the alternative energy unit in her high school environmental science class. She saw the possibility of teaching South African students to design and build their own solar-powered lanterns by using some simple materials they already had access to, such as a glass jar or other clear containers.

In 2012 Pam partnered with Sundance Solar to design a working prototype of a solar-powered LED jar light kit. After a few months, Ed and Pam had a circuit board designed and produced in order to create a functional do-it-yourself kit. The SunBender DIY Solar LED Jar Light Kit is a simple way of turning a recycled jar into a functioning solar lantern and is available to teachers and the general public. Pam also developed a detailed curriculum guide for teachers, home-schoolers, and parents. The guide is available for free on Sundance Solar's website.

One Million Lights

One Million Lights is a nonprofit organization that gives away solar lights around the world. Sundance sells them our SolarLab educational kit that they use in their programs.

Angaza Design

Angaza design has developed a Pay Go system to allow people to buy solar lights spread out over time so they can afford them. They can pay with cash or with their phones.[95] Sundance is working with Angaza and Greenlight Planet to distribute the solar lights with the Angaza technology built-in.

Solar Lights Moving Forward

Ed Bender and Pam Ulicny traveled to South Africa in 2015 to launch the project. They have raised enough money with an Indigogo campaign for the initial order of 200 light kits. There's a calculus between the project as self-sustaining through sales of student-manufactured lights to replace disposable batteries and kerosene and solid fuels, and additional philanthropic donations and funding from government development organizations and NGOs to scale up more quickly.

By using solar to support lights and cell phone charging, the use of cell phone-based Pay Go system provides a workable economic platform that can be generalized. Key for Sundance Solar's Solar Lights project and similar initiatives is to have a successful self-managing model that can be expanded, scaled up, and modified for differing circumstances.

Sundance Solar's projects are one example of the global social and technological context of a renewable world and sustainability rising. Sundance Solar is getting started with the first 200 Sunbender Solar Light kits donated for youth in South African townships in the summer of 2015. Solar Light's future, and all our futures, remains uncertain. Slowly, but surely, the grassroots force of ecological social change is moving. The sun is rising.

Sustainability Speaks Sutra[96]

Sustainability is the evolution of an industrial to an ecological civilization.

⊡

Sustainability is the process of transformation.

⊡

Sustainability is a description of the operation of the biosphere ever tending toward a dynamic balance. Sustainability is thus a biological process with a social resonance and a social process with a biological resonance.

⊡

Sustainability is the melding of change and of continuity. It is the history of evolution of life and the biosphere. It is both the expression and refutation of progress and of method.

⊡

Our future and sustainability's future can never by reliably parsed from existing conditions. Sustainability is rooted in contingency.

⊡

Sustainability is iterative, recursive, endlessly creative and generative. Sustainability is the creature of chaotic dynamics, of broken sets, always of n+1, of emergence of the unknown, unpredictable and transcendent.

⊡

Sustainability is the search for life's continuity and therefore for balance in response to all influences and thus the gate to change. It is the nature of life, the natural inclination of living systems.

◻

Sustainability's nature is life responding to all influences to in a manner that serves to maximize the opportunities for all life as a whole, for the maximum benefit of all species.

◻

Sustainability is a grand co-evolutionary dynamic between life and ecosphere one endlessly shaping the other in the dance of life and the geophysical.

◻

Sustainability is the manifestation of life's history, of the co-evolution of life and ecosphere.

21

Ecological Tax Transformation

Sustainability is the application and expression of an ecological consumption tax system.

Have the Price System Send Signals for Sustainability Through Ecological Consumption Assessments to Replace Income Taxation

Pollution, depletion and ecological damage are the holes in the boat of corporate capitalism in the 21st century. "Externalities" is economist talk for pollution when its consequences are external to the price system, and therefore distort the market. If the polluter and its customers do not have to pay, someone else does, whether on the next block or in future generations. The operation of the market's invisible hand becomes a sleight-of-hand trick lining the pockets of polluters. Today, market distortion from externalities, unless promptly corrected, raises the real prospect for global ecological collapse along with the ruin of the global market system.

For ecological markets to work, what is sustainable must become less expensive, more profitable, and gain market share. What is polluting, depleting, and ecologically damaging must become more expensive, less profitable and loose market share. The price system needs to send clear signals for sustainability to consumers, producers, bankers, investors, and government officials.

Market systems by their nature work well and are sustainable only to the extent that they are able to include all costs in the market price. If costs of pollution are shifted to others—if they are externalized and expected to be paid for by those who are downwind or downstream or by future generations—the market system will reward self-destructive conduct. The ultimate result of self-destructive conduct is self-destruction.

Taxes and Assessments to Eliminate Externalities

Economist Cecil Pigou in his book *The Economics of Welfare* published in 1920 developed a system of so-called Pigovian taxes on externalities, including pollution. Pigou found ways to calculate and optimize the balance between marginal private profits and the marginal social cost of externalities. This is more economist talk meaning a proper balance is struck between the gains of the polluter and the losses of society. The economic affects of the taxes are calibrated to discourage the pollution while its social costs are optimally reduced.

Not only individually, but crucially in the aggregate, the producers, consumers, and investors are encouraged by price signals from Pigovian taxes to reduce pollution and ecological damage and repair the holes in capitalism's boat.

There is, of course, a fundamental problem when applying economic optimization to the possibilities and prospects for the collapse of living systems. In far from equilibrium conditions, living systems are subject to sudden and catastrophic change. The finely wrought optimization equations of economists often do not apply to the complexities of ecology. We have, at best, only partial and fragmentary knowledge of the actual conditions of the ecosphere under stress or an understanding of the consequences of just one more unit of pollution on the margin in living systems whose behavior can suddenly become nonlinear.

While scientists and engineers, when given good models of camels and knowledge of their anatomy, may offer a prediction of what straw will likely break a camel's back, we will not know what is the last pound of carbon dioxide that suddenly moves the climate into sudden and dramatic change

Today, as the market ship continues to take on water and is listing heavily to starboard, it's important to realize that there is both an extensive range of possibilities, as well as limits, for effective Pigovian taxes and assessments. To be clear, the success of an ecological global growth strategy is dependent, in part, on the market price system sending clear signals for sustainability to producers, consumers, and investors. But such signals are meaningful in the context of a fundamental commitment for making economic growth result in ecological improvement, the regeneration of natural capital, and the advancement of ecological justice. Pigovian taxes are means to help send proper signals to help to accomplish the broad goals of a politically and socially chosen ecological global growth agenda. They are not an economic black box that will operate independently and without ongoing adjustment and recalibration delivering magically a sustainable future.

An ecological assessment regime to help catalyze and support an ecological growth agenda must be both comprehensive and designed with appropriate feedback and adjustment mechanisms. Almost a century after Pigou's pioneering work there has been no systematic adoption of Pigovian taxes to seal the leaks in the market ship in a systematic fashion.

Nevertheless there exists a wide range of choices for economists and politicians to develop an effective blend of measures to send strong and clear market signals to end pollution and turn away from the path to self-destruction and to pursue profitable and ecological ends.[97]

The lesson of business and pollution as usual is that instead of developing market fixing taxes on pollution, the last century after Pigou has led to the mushrooming of taxes on income and consumption with little regard to how that income was obtained, or the effects of what is purchased, as long as the tax was paid. Al Capone, for example, was sent to Alcatraz not for murder and racketeering, but for tax evasion.

What's important to understand is that, unfortunately, the existing income and sales tax system is completely compatible with pollution and ecological destruction as usual. And further, the existing progressive income tax that levies higher rates on the rich, is also apparently completely compatible with dramatic increases, both nationally and globally, in inequality. Such realities have apparently not stopped a ceaseless right-wing program to cut income taxes as a means to allegedly stimulate economic growth while it has the effect of reducing government revenue, turning surpluses to deficits, dismantling government programs, and increasing inequality as the rich get much richer, the middle class shrinks, and wages for workers stagnate.

The tax system is broken. It's time to fix it. It's time to seal the holes in the boat and chart of course to pursue economic growth that leads to the regeneration of natural capital and to justice and fairness. This is not just a matter of marginal improvement, but the use of Pigovian taxes in an effective blend to support the broad goals of a transformative ecological global growth agenda. If a tax, fee, or assessment does not serve this end, it should be abandoned or modified for it to send proper market signals before it is too late for the market to have gravely damaged or destroyed itself.

Yes, there are flaws in some Pigovian taxes on consumption, such as their regressive nature. The poor consume almost all of their income, while the rich do not. This flaw can be remedied through measures such as the Basic Income Guarantee (BIG), or Negative Income Tax (NIT), or the Basic Energy Entitlement (BEE). Such measures need to be considered as essential in 21st century tax repair and an ecological global growth strategy. There is no inherently right-wing or left-wing answer for such questions. As we have seen, for example, social justice measures such as some form of a Basic Income Guarantee or Negative Income Tax to replace welfare has broad support across the political spectrum.

It's worth noting that a proper balance of levies on pollution and support for justice and fairness in the 21st century can mean the abolishing of income tax for all and expanding transfer payments to those in need.

22

Assessments on Pollution, Depletion, and Ecological Damage

Sustainability means decreasing pollution increases profit, and increasing pollution, decreases profit.

There is a broad range of Pigovian levies on pollution, depletion, and ecological damage to send clear economic signals that can be placed. The following have penalties:

- Pollution and emissions such as carbon
- Products produced by polluting processes
- Deletion of non-renewable resources
- Income from sources or pollution
- Income from sinks for pollution
- Some or all economic transactions indexed to pollution such as an ecological valued-added tax system
- All consumption has an annual tax that can be indexed in the Computer Age based on the nature of an individual's total annual purchases
- The measurement ecological footprint of any activity
- The cumulative annual ecological footprint of an individual based on purchases
- Ecological condition of land

- ⊚ Levies on extraction and production of all natural resources

- ⊚ Pollution products and "fee-bate" transfer of those revenues to non-polluting competitors lower their costs

- ⊚ Imports whose producing countries do not have similar levies based on pollution, depletion, and ecological damage

Surely, an effective and economically appropriate system can be developed from these fourteen types of Pigovian measures to send proper economic signal to support an ecological global growth agenda. And beyond what I have listed, I am almost sure there are others I have not considered. It's time that consideration of a comprehensive ecological tax system combined with measures for justice and fairness be major political questions.

Europe uses ecological taxes. For example, a sales tax added to gasoline and fuel where revenue collected is targeted to help pay for social insurance. China similarly has adopted a variety of ecological taxes and fees. The basic weakness of such a system of scattered ecological taxes is that they are inherently marginal and depend on the ongoing existence of the polluting item for revenue. What matters is for us to move quickly for tax reform that sends clear and comprehensive market signals for ecological sanity throughout the economy.

Ecological Consumption Assessments

A direct and comprehensive way to send price signals to producers and consumers, that I favor, is through ecological consumption assessments paid at the point of sale on all goods and services throughout the economy—from mine to the department store's and every stage in between. Buy an item that's less polluting than a item of similar quality and you will pay less. This is a variation upon the Value-Added Tax (VAT) transformed into an Ecological

Value-Added Tax or EVAT. This is one comprehensive model.[98] But it certainly cannot the limit of the extensive choices readily available.

A successful model of an ecological value-added tax has been implemented in Brazil (ICMS-Ecológico) to support the development of a sustainable agro-forestry. Local state protectors of land receives an expanded portion of the proceeds of the value-added tax. A similar program has been instituted in Portugal on a national level.[99]

We will examine in detail the nuts and bolts of the operation of ecological consumption assessments by varying EVAT rates that depend on the degree of pollution, depletion, and ecological damage. The greater the amount of ecological damage, the higher the ecological (EVAT) rate.

Ecological Consumption Assessment System

An Ecological Consumption Assessment System is indexed according to the degree of pollution, depletion, and ecological damage of a good or service. Ecological Valued-Added Assessments are paid for at the point of sale for all goods and services and can replace income taxation after the fact. Ecological Value-Added Assessments can make the market an effective instrument for moving the myriad of production, consumption, and investment decisions along sustainable paths. The more sustainable, the lower the Ecological Value-Added Assessment. Simple color codes ranging from deep green to black can distinguish green sustainable goods and services from unsustainable products that will pay higher assessment rates. Assessment rates will be initially assigned by SIC codes by industry and eventually will be product specific, providing lower Ecological Assessment rates and a competitive advantage for sustainable goods and services.

Being a smart businessperson and pursuing a low cost, higher profit path must mean becoming a sustainable business person.

As comprehensive ecological taxes are phased in over a ten-year period, rating each good or service on a simple sustainability scale, income taxes are phased out. Such an ecological consumption assessment system, for the United States, is described in my book, *Markets, Democracy and Survival: How to Be Prosperous Without Being Self-Destructive.*

Replacing much of income taxation, by modifying a VAT based on ecological consumption assessments on all goods and services throughout the economy, will help move economies as a whole toward sustainable paths. A VAT is part of the tax system in almost all advanced industrialized nations other than the United States. The Ecological Valued-Added Assessments type VAT avoids the double taxation of ordinary sales taxes. And since the Ecological Valued-Added Assessments VAT is organized around the credit for invoices system where no tax or, in our case, ecological assessments, will be paid on invoices paid to suppliers, the system is essentially self-enforcing. Business people want to report sales and underlying invoices used to produce goods or services and thereby gain exemption from assessments for the value of their purchases. And most importantly, by its nature, the ecological assessment system encourages business people to reduce their costs and increase their profits by buying sustainable goods to produce their product or service.

Ecological assessments are not simply a tax on pollution, where revenue is dependent upon a bad item of pollution, such as a cigarette tax. It is an assessment on the value of all goods and services based on the level of sustainability. It is best viewed as an assessment on ecological consequences of a good or service instead of a tax levied on income from productive economic activity. The assessment rises as the degree of pollution increases. The assessment falls as the degree of pollution declines.

As unsustainable goods paying the highest assessment are forced from the market, to maintain revenue, the assessment rate on other goods will increase. Eventually, as the economy approaches sustainability as norm, this will mean a flat assessment on most goods and services, with very high assessments on the few remaining polluting outliers. An average ecological assessment in the 20 percent range can replace all income taxes and fund the government through a system that sends profound ecological price signals throughout the economy.

Under an ecological assessment system, smart business and the pursuit of profit will mean sustainable business. The price system can be made to work for us, and not against us.

Sustainability's Zero Discount Rate Sutra[100]

Sustainability means economic growth leading to ecological improvement, not ecological destruction.

☐

Sustainability means decreasing pollution increases profit, and increasing pollution, decreases profit.

☐

Sustainability is the application and expression of an ecological consumption tax system.

☐

Sustainability means the application of a zero discount rate to the future.

23

China and Potential for Ecological Value-Added Taxes

Sustainability is the needed practice of an ecological ethics
that considers as integral the consequence and effects
of all action upon other people and upon the ecosphere.

Sustainability

For China as an exporter, an ecological consumption assessment system will represent the basis for an enduring competitive advantage in a world forced to respond to ecological norms. In compliance with GATT rules, such a tax can be placed on imports from countries that do not impose such a tax domestically.

China is in a particularly good position to take advantage of ecological consumption assessments since the Chinese VAT, Consumption Tax (CT), and Business Tax (BT) already provide a substantial fraction of government revenue.

The current Chinese VAT tax has a basic rate of 17 percent, with a reduced rate of 13 percent for food, fuel, electricity, books, newspapers and magazines, and agricultural products. A zero rate applies to most export goods.

The Business Tax (BT) rate is generally 3 percent to 5 percent, but with some items, like entertainment, up to 20 percent. The BT is a kind of turnover tax imposed on various service and asset transfer income. Unlike a VAT, it does not have a credit for purchases, and therefore the BT cascades through the economy. The BT was being replaced, starting in 2012 and 2013, in some sectors such as transportation, asset leasing, R & D, information technology, radio and TV, and cultural and creative services.

The Consumption Tax (CT) is a classic "sin tax" or luxury tax imposed on fourteen consumable or luxury goods (including cigarettes, alcohol, gasoline, and motor vehicles). CT rates range from 1 percent to 45 percent. Some products are taxed at a fixed amount based on quantity.

China's 3 VAT related taxes were established in 1993 by the P.R.C. State Council. The VAT applies to most goods, but not to services using labor. These are covered by the business tax or BT on services and immovable property. Together the Chinese VAT and BT cover ground similar to the classic European VAT. Goods and services in China are subject to either the VAT or the BT, not both. The third tax, the Consumption Tax or CT, is a typical luxury tax.

VAT currently applies to the sale of goods, the importation of goods, and the provision of repair, replacement and processing services in China. VAT in China exhibits some of the features of other VAT regimes throughout the world with some particular Chinese characteristics. China's VAT taxes final private consumption spending (as well as some public spending) and properly maintains the burden of VAT on transactions between businesses through the input tax credit mechanism.

The classic European VAT, employing the credit for invoices system, functions as a smart sales tax that avoids double taxation. The Chinese VAT system (combining the VAT the Business Tax (BT) and Consumption Tax (CT) according to Xu Yan (2011) differs substantially from the classic VAT in that it is production-based rather than consumption-based, is differentially applied, and in the interest of revenue it allows double taxation by forbidding credit for purchases of some capital goods.

Xu Yan finds:

> . . . the tax is not consistently charged and collected on all transactions by businesses throughout the production and distribution process. Differentiation between general and

small-scale taxpayers results in inconsistent treatment . . . disparities in VAT payment and deduction rates exist for different sectors. The 1994 VAT regulations did not allow for
deduction of input tax on capital investment. Capital-inten-
sive industries would suffer a comparatively higher VAT burden than labor-intensive industries. Finally, China's VAT is
not neutral in that it is formally administered on a destination
basis, though rebates of input taxes are variable by sector and
commodity. . . . Like most other countries, China normally
uses zero rating for exports, but the government frequently
adjusts the rates at which input taxes are credited or rebated
on exports.[101]

Whatever its faults, the Chinese VAT system is a substantial revenue raiser. The National Bureau of Statistics in China reported
that in 2008 the combined VAT family (not including taxes on
imports) raised about 50 percent of total revenue.[102]

The transformation to an ecological value-added tax system
will assist China in becoming global leader in pursuit of an ecological global growth agenda.

In June 2015, China Legislative Affair's Office issued a draft
environmental taxation law on air, water, noise, and solid waste
pollution that includes specific rates on pollutants. According to
Jia Kang, head of the Ministry of Finance's Research Institute for
Fiscal Science, "Purely relying on traditional administrative inter-
ventions is clearly no longer adequate to deal with the current
problems."[103]

Taxation is combined with the new law adopted on January
1st imposing criminal and civil penalties on polluters, along with
President Xi's announcement of harsh penalties on corrupt Party
officials.

SUSTAINABILITY AND THE BIOSPHERE'S SYSTEM STATE SUTRA[104]

Sustainability is the planet's practice of dynamic equilibrium.

◘

Sustainability is an expression of the system state of the biosphere.

◘

Sustainability is a property of the ecosphere. Sustainability can refer to and attempt to be measured and quantified and described by such as ecosystem services, carrying capacity, and ecological footprint, but it is not reducible to any single measure or a bundle of measures.

◘

Sustainability can be practiced by, and has been practiced by, a broad range of social and economic systems. It is incompatible with the self-destructive conduct of industrial business as usual. But sustainability is also the expression of excess creating a countervailing and healing response. This too is sustainability.

◘

Sustainability is the needed practice of an ecological ethics that considers as integral the consequence and effects of all action upon other people and upon the ecosphere.

◘

Sustainability is 21st century science and systems theory and practice.

◘

Sustainability is the attempt to account for and optimize the consequences of all human action.

◘

Sustainability is the awareness that we can no more predict all the consequences of our actions upon one another and upon the biosphere, than a physicist can measure the speed of an electron without effecting its position.

◘

Sustainability is the awareness of our power and vulnerability, ultimately harmonizing the dynamic balance of human lightness and darkness, of the one and the many, of freedom and community.

◘

Sustainability is the awareness and dynamic balance of human power and human vulnerability. Sustainability is the emergent social practice and social theory of the 21st century, guiding and impelling the transformation of an industrial to an ecological civilization.

24

India: The Renewable Energy Imperative

Sustainability is an emergent property of an ecological civilization expressing the transformation from industrial to ecological civilization.

Bangladesh and India are a study in contrasts. India is huge, economically dynamic, and chose in 2015 to be a global leader in PV development. Bangladesh is much smaller, poorer, and is planning, with Indian investment, to pursue coal and liquefied natural gas as the solutions to its energy needs.

India Goes All In on Solar PV

India Prime Minister Narendra Modi of the conservative BJP went all-in on solar energy in 2015. India is planning to install 100,000 megawatts of solar PV by 2022. This is around ten times more capacity then the planned fossil fuel expansion in Bangladesh supported by investment by Indian conglomerates.

India's enormous PV effort is hitting the ground running.[105] In January 2015 the Adani conglomerate, the same group to invest in fossil fuel in Bangladesh, announced a 4 billion dollar investment with Sun Edison in a new, huge Indian PV manufacturing plant. The new giant SunEdison-Ajani PV manufacturing plant to be built in India will help drive down PV costs to $1.00-$1.25 per watt or even below $1.00.

"This facility will create ultra-low cost solar panels that will enable us to produce electricity so cost effectively it can compete head to head, unsubsidized and without incentives, with fossil fuels," said Ahmad Chatila, President and Chief Executive Officer of US-based Sun Edison.[106]

SunEdison and First Solar of the United States are already major players in India. Canadian Solar, based in Canada but with Chinese manufacturing, and China's JA solar and JinkoSolar are planning major investments in India.

First Solar, for example, is installing utility scale PV in India and supplying electricity costs substantially less at $.10–$15 cent per kWh compared to diesel generation costing $.25 per kWh or more. The capital cost of utility scale PV is now down to $1.50 per megawatt and continuing to decline. This means 1,000 megawatts of PV could be built today for $1.5 billion to provide power for twenty-five years or more with zero fuel costs and modest maintenance expense. This is power that's cheaper than competing fossil fuel generation.

India, and its conservative government, is clearly opening the door wide to become a global leader in the building of a renewable energy future and an ecological global growth strategy. There's much more to come from India.

25

Bangladesh:
Problems and Opportunities

Sustainability as an emergent property is an expression of nonlinear processes and evolutionary dynamics.

Bangladesh is a typical example of the energy and environmental problems and opportunities of the world's poor nations. It lacks capital. It is particularly vulnerable to the consequences of climate change and ecological disruption. Its energy infrastructure, both fossil fuel and renewables, is generally poorly developed. The bright spot is a world-leading program of installing small-scale solar energy, led by Grameen Shakti, in areas without electric grid power. But this success is viewed more as a stop-gap than the basis for efficient renewable development that avoids the well-worn path of high-pollution fossil fuel development.

Profile of Bangladesh

Bangladesh is a very poor country of 150 million with GDP per capita of $957 compared to the US $53,042 GDP per capita according to the World Bank. Bangladesh has an area of 51,000 square miles and a population density of 2,850 people per square mile compared to the United States density of 84 people per square mile.

Most of the land in Bangladesh is less then ten meters above sea level and much of the costal south is at sea level. As such, Bangladesh is particularly vulnerable to rising sea levels from climate change and the effect of intensified typhoons and disastrous flooding.

In 2013 the World Bank warned that a two degree centigrade rise in global temperature particularly threatened Bangladesh with "extreme river floods, more intense tropical cyclones, rising sea levels and very high temperatures." It's estimated that a one meter sea rise, quite likely by the end of the century, would flood 25 percent of the country. [107]

India, adjacent to densely populated and vulnerable areas like Khulna, Satkhira, and Bagerhat, and mindful of the potential for millions of the desperate poor fleeing to higher ground, has built a double-walled, eight foot high barbed wire fence along the border. The so-called "Great Wall of India" now covers 70 percent of the 2,544 mile border with Bangladesh.[108]

Electricity in Bangladesh

Only about 60 percent of people in Bangladesh have grid power, and the average energy use per capita is miniscule compared to the United States. Bangladesh has become a world leader in establishment of small-scale solar energy for homes without electric power. Led by Grameen Shakti, 80,000 or more homes a month are having small solar panels installed to power a couple of LED lights as part of a program to bring renewables, job income, and affordable credit and banking to the rural poor.[109]

Unfortunately, while Bangladesh is a leader in small solar, the power grid relies on natural gas and coal, and plans for future development are to rely on new coal, natural gas, and nuclear energy in an expending gird. Solar and wind is planned to play only a small part in this development, despite very large solar potential and substantial offshore wind resources in the Bay of Bengal.[110]

The power grid has a peak of about 7,500 megawatts. Current plans are to double or triple electrical capacity using "affordable" coal, natural gas, and nuclear energy. The Bangladesh Power System National Plan of 2010 looks to expand the electric gird and increase capacity to 30,000 megawatts or more. The chief of power planning opined that to meet the nation's power need with solar would mean covering the whole country with PV panels.

In fact, an area just 18 miles by 18 miles (or 256 square miles) would generate sufficient electricity for all Bangladesh's needs if supported by storage resources. This amounts just to one half of one percent of total land area.[111]

NREL (National Renewable Energy Laboratory) estimates that PV potential in Bangladesh is 380,000,000 megawatt hours of power. This is several times the output of current 7,500 megawatts of mostly fossil fuel operating at 75 percent capacity factor, about 50,000 megawatt hours.

Realistically, a combination of offshore wind, distributed solar, solar farm developments, and development of copious biomass and gasification resources could move Bangladesh on a sustainable pathway both economically and ecologically.

Wind has similar or greater cost advantages than new solar from mega factories. Capital costs of offshore wind currently has an average of $4.30 a watt. The shallow Bay of Bengal sites are likely in the lower $3.25 a watt range. New wind farms have 50 percent capacity factor, which makes unsubsidized wind power cost competitive with fossil since there is zero fuel cost. One thousand megawatts of offshore wind should cost around $3.5 billion.

But the reality of the politics of energy development in Bangladesh has made it possible to buy foreign coal and nuclear plants and continue to rely on natural gas.

Bangladesh could and should be considered as a very practical text case for the pursuit and finance of the renewable path for the poor in the global south. But now, instead of planning to develop a few thousand megawatts of offshore wind, plans for only a couple of hundred megawatts is moving ahead very slowly. Instead of planning a few thousand megawatts of solar PV and storage resources, there is little PV planned beyond the admirable small-scale electrification. Likewise, there is little development of copious gasification resources from manure and biomass for electric generation.

Now for the future of Bangladesh there are coal, nukes, and natural gas instead of PV power and wind power from India. In summary, 11,000 megawatts of coal, nuclear energy, and natural gas power are to be built for a nation that is one of the most threatened by climate change.

Fossil Fuel Plans for Bangladesh

Five 1,200 megawatt coal-fired, ultra-critical power plants are planned. The first is to be built jointly by the Bangladesh Power Development Board (BPDB) and a Chinese company, The Matoaboro coal plant in Chittagong, features Japanese loan capital and development of a deep sea port to handle the import of soft coal. A 2,000 megawatt Rooppur Nuclear plant is in the cards, as is an LNG import plant in partnership with India to power a 3,000 megawatt natural gas plant, and convert Maheshkhali Island in the Bay of Bengal into the country's largest fossil-fuel energy hub.

The Rampal coal plant is to be built near the Sundarbans, the world's largest mangrove forest and last refuge for the remaining 270 Bengal tigers. The plant received environmental approval aided by a regulatory light of hand that classified the mangroves as rural farmland.[112]

And, in June 2015, immediately following a welcome June 2015 deal resolving decades old border disputes between India and Bangladesh, Indian conglomerates Reliance and Adani announced plans to invest five billion dollars in Bangladesh's fossil fuel power sector, just before a visit to Dhaka by Indian Prime Minister Narendra Modi.

The announced targets are the 3,000 megawatt liquefied natural gas project, and the 1,600 megawatt coal plant for the island of Maheshkhali. "The MOUs will be signed tomorrow," said PDB chairman Shahinul Islam Khan, adding that "the deals are non-binding and are still in primary stage."[113]

While the officials of Bangladesh plan to recapitulate the errors of the 20th century in the 21st century and India goes all-in on solar, the government of Hawaii has also just passed a renewable portfolio standard requiring that 100 percent of Hawaii's energy by 2050 will come from renewables combing solar, wind, geothermal, and tidal power to power a densely populated island chain using substantial amounts of energy.

Bangladesh with still small energy demand and substantial renewable resources is a perfect place to demonstrate the ability to design, finance, and implement an efficient renewable transformation.

Instead there's still money to be made and capital to be had in pursuit of the high pollution fossil fuel dead end whose consequences for Bangladesh will be rising seas of the Bay of Bengal that will cover the land already at sea level that is home for many millions of the poor.

Sustainability As an Emergent Property of the Ecosphere[114]

Sustainability is ever in motion, ever subject to modification, a reflection of a universal principle of ceaseless co-evolution and change.

◙

Sustainability is an expression of the ecosphere. The ecosphere can no more be separated from the earth than humanity can be from the ecosphere. Even in a spaceship we are bringing our atmosphere and water and food with us.

◙

Sustainability can and must be applied to all aspects of human conduct. An industrial ecology is not an oxymoron; it is the application of sustainability to products and manufacturing.

Sustainability is an emergent property of an ecological civilization expressing the transformation from industrial to ecological civilization.

◙

Sustainability as an emergent property is a reflection of the industrial system-state giving rise to new levels of organization and behavior, much as crystal structures suddenly emerge from a supersaturated solution to find new equilibrium, or solid matter cohering from a sufficient quantity of atoms in a quantum state. Sustainability, at bottom, rests upon the sudden appearance of new things.

◘

Sustainability as an emergent property is an expression of nonlinear processes and evolutionary dynamics.

◘

What we can say is that life is an emergent quality or expression of the physical world. And sustainability represents an emergent quality of the biosphere toward the maintenance of a dynamic balance suitable for life.

◘

Emergence is the appearance of new properties and levels of organization given constituents of sufficient quantity and quality. Crystal structures, for instance, are an emergent property of certain minerals in supersaturated solutions. Solid matter is an emergent quality of a large numbers atoms existing in a quantum state. And life and the earth shaping biosphere represents a grand expression of emergence.

◘

Emergence is the polar opposite of reductionism. The truths behind sustainability are not found by the examination of smaller and smaller parts. Rather, the emergence of sustainability is the tale told by the interaction of the one and the many, of the forest and the trees, of the fish and the sea.

26

Bangladesh and Louisiana: A Cautionary Tale

Our social life, the rise of second nature, is both an expression of sustainability and now becomes a self-conscious instrument of sustainability.

Bangladesh in some ways resembles New Orleans and Louisiana. In New Orleans, the poorer you are, particularly if you're African American, you are likely to live at or below sea level. The Lower Ninth Ward, devastated by hurricane Katrina, is well below sea level. When the poorly constructed levee broke under the force of the storm surge, a wall of water swept away the houses of the Lower Ninth.

The storm surge had followed MRGo (Mississippi River Gulf Outlet Canal) from the Gulf that was built to make it easier and convenient to move oil and cargo to and from the Gulf. MRGo has also proven particularly useful to allow hurricane storm surges to follow unimpeded toward the Mississippi and Lake Ponchartrain and into the levees protecting New Orleans. The marshes and bayou that protected New Orleans and the coast from hurricanes had already been systematically degraded and pierced by oil and gas pipelines and canals with MRGo providing the perfect coup de grâce.

I was taken on a Katrina tour of New Orleans by the Louisiana State Climatologist that included the Lower Ninth, its levees, and MRGo. Glorious patches of weeds and an occasional vegetable garden now fill the abandoned lots in the Lower Ninth along with small clusters of new solar homes for Lower Ninth residents built by Make It Right with funding assistance by Brad Pitt.

Population in the Lower Ninth in 2000 was 14,000. The next census, in 2010, after Katrina, counted 3,000. In 2015 there were still no grocery or drug stores nine years after Katrina hit the Lower Ninth. There is one school, and talk of luxury condos that may or may not be built on the site of a bulldozed school destroyed by Katrina.[115] This is a cautionary tale from the Lower Ninth, for Bangladesh, and for all of us of the consequences of continuing to follow the fossil fuel path.

The Garden of Life Sutra[116]

Sustainability is the growth and development of the garden of life. Sustainability is the purposeless purpose, the intention-less intent. Sustainability is the expression of the myriad interactions between life and ecosphere. Sustainability now encompasses human self-consciousness and social action.

◙

Sustainability is an expression of all levels of life's ability to maintain its integrity, as an eddy of self-organization within the ecosphere, embraced and fed by the ecosphere with the ability not only to maintain itself, but to reproduce itself and to change, to evolve in ways that also conditions and changes the biosphere in the interest of conditions favorable for life.

◙

The ecosphere by its character and therefore its nature is an expression of the dynamics of sustainability. From your local woodland pond, to the planet as a whole, as Gaea, the ecosphere tends to maintain a dynamic balance. This dynamic balance is a response to and the sum of all influences. There is no lifeless zone on our planet. Somehow, life helps make and maintain the entire planet and its diverse ecosystems as suitable homes for life and its diverse, ever changing forms.

◙

Our planet, over some billions of years of existence, has been shaped by a grand process of coevolution of life and of Earth. Life and the earth as it exists can be considered a single expression of being. They are inseparable.

Sustainability is therefore an emergent property of the biosphere as a totality, as Gaea, and thus a natural phenomenon that reflects the sum total of all activity. Sustainability is always being approached and ever slipping away.

We do not know why this grand co-evolution of life and Earth is so. Why and how has life appeared and evolved in way that somehow coordinates its behaviors and interactions with other creatures and the biosphere to create and maintain conditions hospitable for life? Is this an expression of the divine, or spirit? Is it a universal tendency? Is it a singular expression of unique circumstances? Is it simply a reflection of where we have been and a window upon where we may be going? It is what it is. It could be no other way. It is majestic and breath taking. We are a part of it and as self-conscious beings now have a responsibility to contribute as individuals and as community to its well-being.

And sustainability, the maintenance of a dynamic balance in response to change, is also the basis for evolution and further change. This is one of the underlying facts of life. Our planet is a vital entity. Continents move. Volcanoes erupt. Ice advances and retreats. Sea levels rise and fall. The climate and the atmosphere change. Sometimes great waves of extinction sweep over the planet as a new homeostatic balance is established in response to all influences upon the ecosphere.

⊡

Sustainability and evolution are complementary dynamics supporting change and survival. Evolution is a sustainability mechanism. Sustainability sits on the stool of evolution. Without evolutionary mechanisms, sustainability would fail, and the web of life collapse. Evolution is a necessary attribute of sustainability by which life assures its survival in response to ever changing circumstances. But evolution is also a two way street. The earth changes organisms, and organisms also change the earth.

⊡

Since the rate of change varies, so does the rhythm of evolutionary change. As the rate and degree of environmental change varies, there is a corresponding variance in the speed of evolution, the creation of new species, and the pace of extinction. This is the punctuated nature of evolutionary change described by biologist Steven J. Gould.

⊡

Evolution is not limited to random genetic mutation and Darwinian selection, but also incorporates mechanisms of genetic exchange—for example, of bacteria exposed to antibiotics and of symbiosis, such as mitochondria that is essential for energy metabolism, once independent creatures become resident in the cells of complex organisms, including people.

⬚

We have been poorly served by the reductionist habit of science that has ignored the fundamentally co-evolutionary relationship between life and ecosphere and instead is focused, for example, on mechanisms of random gene variation, reduced by some to the triumph of selfish genes in an evolutionary marketplace governed like a marketplace by an invisible hand transmuting selfish striving to the common good.

⬚

Sustainability is the nows manifesting the thens.

⬚

Sustainability is an expression of life; life is an expression of sustainability.

⬚

Our social life, the rise of second nature, is both an expression of sustainability and then becomes a self-conscious instrument of sustainability.

⬚

Our ability to account for all forces contributing to the sustainable, let alone our ability to quantify them, is necessarily extraordinarily limited. We approach sustainability from the position of a man in the midst of a blazing inferno he has ignited, and who is attempting to consider the health of the meadow now being consumed.

◫

Sustainability cannot be observed by an isolated observer. The attempt to reduce sustainability will mean acting as a participant, and therefore changing, to an unknown extent, the course sustainability in action. Sustainability is an expression of contingency, communication, and cybernetic feedback. The sum total of myriad instabilities and acts can appear as the expression of the steady state.

27
Global Tour:
Places Working to Get It Right

Sustainability is thus a mitigating increase in social complexity to solve seemingly insoluble problems of industrialism and industrial reductionism.

California Utilities to Spend $1 Billion on Electric Car Charging Stations

Pacific Gas & Electric (PG&E) plans to build 25,000 level-two charging stations and 100 DC fast charge stations for $653.8 million. Southern California Edison's Charge Ready Program would build 31,500 charging stations by 2020 for $355 million. San Diego Gas and Electric's $103 million electric vehicle grid integration will test customer response to variable charging rates by installing 550 charging stations by 2025.[117]

The future of a renewable energy transition will include the transition to electric vehicles both to displace oil with massive battery storage resource to dramatically lower energy costs, and dramatically lower pollution, depletion, and ecological damage. California is in the lead in the number of electric vehicles offering electric vehicle rates, and now also in building electric vehicle charging infrastructure.

In addition to charging stations, most EV users charge at home at night and should be able to take advantage of access to special charging rates, encouraging use of off-peak night time electricity that can be supplied by wind, hydro tidal power, and geothermal in a renewable grid system.

EV owners in PG&E's territory can charge their vehicles at night for the equivalent of about $1 per gallon. A calculator on PG&E's website lets drivers compare costs of driving with different vehicles, under traditional residential rate plans and various EV rate options. A separate meter keeps EV charging costs separate from the rest of your home. In the United States 21 million utility customers now have access to such rates in the United States with 25 percent living in California's PG&E territory. California leads.[118]

Vermont House Bill 40 Mandates 55 Percent Renewables by 2017 and 75 Percent by 2032

Vermont Governor Peter Shumlin signed House Bill 40[119] in 2015 giving utilities incentives to increase their use of renewables while cutting residential greenhouse gas emissions followed the recommendations of the Vermont Public Service Commission 2014 Total Energy Study. The law legalizes solar leasing in Vermont and on-bill financing to facilitate home energy efficiency improvements like high-efficiency air source heat pumps to replace oil and natural gas for home heating.

"The fundamental conclusion of this Total Energy Study is that Vermont can achieve its greenhouse gas emission reduction goals and its renewable energy goals while maintaining or increasing Vermont's economic prosperity. However, to do so will require significant changes in energy policy, fuel supply, infrastructure, and technology."[120]

Hawaii to Go 100 Percent Renewables

In spring 2015, by an overwhelming vote, Hawaii passed legislation HB 623, requiring the state to generate 100 per cent of its electricity from renewables by 2045. Today 80 percent of Hawaii's power is from expensive fossil fuel. Hawaii will be the first US state to completely decarbonize its electricity. Hawaii Electric had already planned to increase renewables to forty percent by 2030.

"As the first state to move toward 100 percent renewable energy, Hawaii is raising the bar for the rest of the country. Local renewable projects are already cheaper than liquid natural gas and oil, and our progress toward meeting our renewable energy standards has already saved local residents hundreds of millions on their electric bills," [121] said Chris Lee, Chairman of the House Energy and Environmental Protection Committee and introducer of HB 623.

Chile: PV Market Without Subsidies Thrives

In 2014 Chile, with 186 megawatts of grid-connected solar power and hundreds more under construction, became the first large scale PV market without either subsidies or feed-in-tariffs.

A combination of great solar conditions, high and variable electric prices, a poor national grid for some sections, declining PV prices, and increasing efficiency open the door for solar without subsidies. Sun Power, for example, is building a 70 megawatt merchant power plant. The Atacama desert offers outstanding solar irradiance of 3,500 watts per square meter, about triple that of most of Germany.

Solar power is either sold into the grid at spot prices hourly with no price floor, particularly in areas where peaking power at supply nodes is very high, or through conventional Purchase Power Agreements that set a long-term price for PV power without subsidies. The Chilean merchant model is likely to be widely duplicated.[122]

The PV future was assisted, as well, by the cancellation of a planned massive HidroAysén mega-dam project on two of Patagonia's wildest rivers, long opposed by citizens and environmentalists. Sustainability is accomplished not just by accepting change, but by making hard choices every step of the way.

Japan: Top Runner Efficiency Standards

Started in 1999, Japan's Top Runner energy efficiency standards now encompass 23 product categories. Unlike standards set by bureaucratic fiat, Top Runner standards are determined by the most efficient product that is given the designation of Top Runner award for it's category and that competitors must attempt to match or exceed. Energy efficiency and innovation becomes a clear competitive advantage in competition for market share.

Only products that meet the energy efficiency standard receive a Top Runner label. Those which do not are labeled differently. Companies try to make ever more efficient models to compete for the award of Japan's 'Top Runner' and gain market share.

The Minister of the Environment (METI) reports the names of companies that fail to meet Top Runner targets and issue recommendations, orders, and fines. So far date, no enforcement actions have ever been ordered, as targets have been systematically met or exceeded.

Top Runner is a good model for systematic global adoption to drive efficiency and to help make economic growth mean ecological improvement. It also suggests inclusion of other standards, such as sustainable content, zero pollution–zero waste to help drive the competitive market place toward sustainability.[123]

Indonesia Forestry Moratorium

In 2015 Indonesia President Joko "Jokowi" Widodo extended the forestry moratorium, designed to protect an area of tropical forests the size of Japan. Indonesia has half of the world's tropical peat swamps, a enormous reservoir of stored carbon and methne, and the third largest tropical forest.[124]

Indonesia also ranked second among tropical nations in forest loss and is a leading greenhouse gas emitter as a result of deforestation and peat land being drained, logged, and burned. Energy use amounts to only about 20 percent of Indonesia greenhouse gas emissions.

Deforestation and habitat destruction has been driven by global demand for tropical hard wood and palm oil produced form plantations on deforested land.

The moratorium, instituted in May 2011 by President Bambang Susilo Yudhoyono has helped the forest, and its renewal is of great importance if Indonesia is able to pursue a sustainable path

The 412 Local Districts have primary responsibility for what happens in the forest in Indonesia. World Resources Institute and partners examined the status of six key reforms and found progress is limited to provinces or districts selected by the Indonesian government as pilot sites, such as Central Kalimantan. Future success must mean good practices must spread nationally from the successful pilot sites.[125]

Arief Yuwono, the Environment and Forestry Ministry Deputy for Degradation and Climate Change said, "We will not erase previous government initiatives that have been good. We will strengthen them."[126] The government will use the forestry law, the plantation law, the disaster management law, the spatial planning law, and the law on protection and management of peat ecosystems.

In Newark New Jersey:
The World's Largest Vertical Farm

Under construction in a converted steel mill in Newark is what will be the world's largest vertical farm. Using a new aeorponic technology the 69,000 square foot facility plans to produce large amounts of greens and herbs.

AeroFarms says its approach accelerates the growth cycle and is 75 times more productive per square foot annually than traditional farms and uses over 95 percent less water. It will have the capacity to grow up to 2 million pounds (910,000 kg) of baby leafy greens and herbs every year to be sold to the local market, thereby cutting transport costs and energy use. The aeroponics approach eliminates peticideds and uses water mist sprayed to deliver nutrients and water to the plants, thus both maximizing bass mass production and using much less water in a closed loop irrigation system. The plants are grown on cloth. Light is provided by LEDs delivering wavelength designed to maximize photosynthesis. The modular stacks for plant growing makes the system high scalable.[127]

Finance is through a public-private partnership funded by the City of Newark, the New Jersey Economic Development Authority (NJEDA), Goldman Sachs, United Fund Advisors, Dudley Ventures, and Prudential Financial.

Obviously, the use of PV and other renewable power to provide the energy for the lights and pumps is part of long-term sustainability.

A sustainable future can mean the renaissance of new farms to produce food near where people live with much less energy and water use than conventional industrial agricultural methods. As a local organic gardener, urban aeroponics doesn't make my heart sing. But neither does the existing high polluting, high resource use, low wage agricultural system. Aeroponics deserves watching and consideration as a sustainable community activity.

Copenhagen: District Sustainability Planning

Copenhagen is one of the world's most pleasant and apparently happy cities. When my son, Sam Schaffer-Morrison, spent his junior year abroad there studying environmental science he was struck that in Copenhagen parents leave their children in baby carriages outside of stores unattended when they went into shop, a behavior that is completely foreign to Americans, but is normal in Denmark's largest city where much effort has been made to improve the quality of life.

Since 2007 District level sustainability planning has made sustainability a central matter of local concern. The 14 sustainability considerations adopted by the city council is the basis for the "sustainability analysis" to create a location based framework for planning and the dialogue with developers.[128] Sustainability considerations addressing the surroundings of the project are relevant to how the project will be developed. This may mean, for example, that the traffic infrastructure and urban space concerns play a decisive role in the development.[129]

The broader context is Copenhagen's plan of becoming the first carbon neutral capital by 2025, supported by a municipal strategic climate action plan of 50 specific initiatives. Each initiative meets the 2015 midterm goal of a 20 percent CO-2 reduction.

Copenhagen's plans have improved the quality of life as well as ecological measurements. Traffic congestion has decreased dramatically through integrated transit and cycling planning. Every day, cyclists travel 1.2 million kilometers in the city. Cleaning the harbor has created attractive living areas, created jobs, and increased tax revenue. Only 1.8 percent of waste now goes to landfills, while the combustion portion heat 98 percent of the city through a district heating system. District cooling systems using seawater from the harbor and surplus heat from the district heating systems through an absorption system is providing increasing amounts of much lower carbon dioxide producing cooling. Copenhagen is a good model for what cities can become in the 21st century.

SUSTAINABILITY IN
THE 21ST CENTURY SUTRA[130]

Sustainability offers the prospect for countervailing and healing ecological change in response to industrial excess.

Sustainability is thus a mitigating increase in social complexity to solve seemingly insoluble problems of industrialism and industrial reductionism.

Sustainability in the 21st century is often invoked and sought, but seldom achieved. Sustainability is presented to us as something new. But this is strange.

As basic a planetary feature as the atmosphere, rich in oxygen and with just enough carbon dioxide, is a product of this co-evolution of life and of Earth. The atmosphere is not a timeless geologic feature. The atmosphere is ever-renewed and sustained by the ecosphere, by plant photosynthesis consuming carbon dioxide and releasing oxygen, and by animal respiration consuming oxygen and releasing carbon dioxide. This is what we learn now in grade school. Perhaps it is heard so often that we cannot appreciate the significance of this truth. Or perhaps the meaning, following the rhythms of Gaea, takes many generations to again pervade consciousness and be expressed as behavior.

◧

What's different about sustainability in the 21st century is that humanity's conduct of industrial business as usual has presented a new series of influences to the biosphere that is changing the climate, destroying habitat, draining aquifers, poisoning land, air, and water with toxic effluents.

◧

Sustainability in the 21st century thus encompasses both social and biological processes. Sustainability is now twofold. This is the source of confusion and difficulty in definition and understanding. As biological process, sustainability and its evolutionary implications must and will include the sum of all human influences upon the biosphere. A great global wave of species extinction now underway is one expression of human influence.

◧

Sustainability is very much within the realm of human behavior and volition. The conduct of industrial civilization has been predicated upon the belief that the social had become master of the biological. This, of course, is a fundamental expression of hubris and the path toward self-destruction. Sustainability is therefore the process of bringing human activity within the self-correcting and balancing ambit of the ecosphere. Thus, in broad compass, sustainability is the inter-action of biological and social evolution. As human social practice, in the long run, sustainability is the process of evolution from an industrial to an ecological civilization.

◻

Sustainability is very much about building an ecological democracy and making the market send accurate price signals for sustainability. What's nonpolluting must cost less and increase profits. What's polluting must cost more and decrease profits.

◻

Our democracy and our market system must make economic growth mean ecological improvement, not ecological destruction. This is the practical definition for sustainability in the 21st century.

◻

The very good news is that we do not have to change ourselves. We do not have to abolish greed and conspicuous consumption. We do have to change our market rules so that we transform the connection between economic growth and the ecosphere. We have it in our power to make the growth in income mean an improvement in the health of the ecosphere and of natural capital. This will not be an easy task. It will require trillions of dollars of productive investment and create enormous positive cash flows and enlist the create efforts and energies of us all.

○

Sustainability in the 21st century will mean we can consume information in all its myriad forms from a renewably powered cyberspace and information manifest as material produced, that is, printed from information using sustainable materials governed by an industrial ecology of zero pollution and zero waste in a world where agriculture, aquaculture, and forestry follow similar ecological norms and ecological market rules.

○

The contours of that ecological democracy and the nature of those new market rules and price signals is our challenge. Sustainability, and therefore the future of our civilization and perhaps the survival of the human species, is at stake.

○

The pursuit of sustainability is the path toward doing good and well. It does not demand perfection, but self-conscious action and the artful dance and feedback of continuous correction.

Notes

Introduction

1. Giles Parkinson, "Solar at Grid Parity in Most of World by 2017," *Renew-Economy*, Australia (January 12, 2015).

2. Seb Henbest et al., *New Energy Outlook Outlook 2015: Powering A Changing World*, Bloomberg L. P. (New York: 2015). http://www.bloomberg.com/company/new-energyoutlook/.

3. Herman K. Trabish, "How the global fuel mix will transform itself over the next 25 years," *Utility Dive* (2015). http://www.utilitydive.com/news/how-the-global-fuel-mix-will-transform-itself-over-the-next-25-years/401806/.

4. Joshua S. Hill, "US & Brazil Pledge Jointly to Raise Renewable Energy to 20% By 2030," *Clean Technica* (2015). http://cleantechnica.com/2015/07/01/us-brazil-pledge-jointly-raise-renewable-energy-20-2030/.

Mass Extinctions

Mass extinction and epochal change is part of life's symphony over the past 500 million years.

5. Charles Q. Choi, "Greatest Mysteries: What Causes Mass Extinctions? Live Science (2007). http://www.livescience.com/1752-greatest-mysteries-mass-extinctions.html.

6. Science2.0.com, News Staff, "Juramaia Sinensis: 160-Million-Year-Old Fossil Pushes Back Mammal Evolution," Science 2.0, August 24, 2011). http://www.science20.com/news_articles/juramaia_sinensis_160million-yearold_fossil_pushes_back_mammal_evolution-81971.

"*Juramaia sinensis,* the earliest known placental mammal, our shrew like ancestor, lived in what is now north east China amidst the dinosaurs 165 million years ago. And yet, mass extinction has meant that groups of species that dominated the earth like the plant-eating dinosaur sauropods and flesh eating theropods, were wiped out 65 million years ago in the extinction at the end of the Cretaceous period, survived only by their avian descendants into the Age of Mammals in the last 65 million years. As climate swiftly changed and the dinosaurs and pterosaurs died, the small shrew-like mammals living amidst the dinosaurs did not. Our genus *Homo* appears in Africa 2.5 million years ago, and *Homo sapiens* existed 200,000 years ago. All of us are maternal descendants of Mitochondrial Eve who lived in East Africa about 150,000 years ago. Our history is part of a grand living and ceaseless evolutionary canvas where we now play a leading role."

7 Vandava Shiva, *Making Peace with the Planet* (London: Pluto Press, 2012).

8. Strategos, "A Bomber an Hour: Lean Manufacturing circa 1944. Strategos Inc. (2014)
http://www.strategosinc.com/willow_run.htm.

A B-24 Bomber an Hour at Willow Run Plant

"In January of 1940, America was being drawn into the growing war and our military was woefully unprepared. The Roosevelt administration asked Ford Motor Company to manufacture components for the B-24 Liberator bomber.

Charles Sorensen, Vice-President of Production for Ford traveled to San Diego to observe Consolidated Aircraft's operations. Here is his description of the visit and how he conceived the Willow Run bomber plant that eventually manufactured 8,800 of these aircraft.

Willow Run was the physical embodiment of the Ford Production system, which was later transformed by Toyota into "Just In Time" and Lean manufacturing. This is where it all started."

9. Shell Global, *New Lens Scenario* (2015). Shell.com. Online:
http://www.shell.com/global/future-energy/scenarios/new-lens-scenarios.html.
http://reneweconomy.com.au/2015/solar-grid-parity-world-2017.

10. Steve Friess, "Inside Suburu's Zero Waste Factory" *Take Part* (2013).
http://www.takepart.com/article/2013/12/30/inside-subarus-zero-waste-factory.

11. Jennifer Goodman, "Lennar Launches No-Cost Solar Program," *Builder* (2014).
http://www.builderonline.com/building/building-science/lennar-launches-no-cost-solar-program_o.

12. Otto Ednhofer and Hermann Lotze-Campe, "Emissions Must Have a Price" (2008) in *Climate Change and Poverty: A Challenge for a Fair World Policy* (2008). Potsdam Institute. Munich, Germany.
https://www.pik-potsdam.de/services/infodesk/books brochures/books/climate-change-and-poverty.

13. Wolfgang Sachs, ed., *The Development Dictionary* (London: Zed Books, 1992).

CHAPTER 1.
Louisiana Then and Now

14. Common Dreams, "Gulf Oil Sickness Wrecking Lives," *Common Dreams* (Oct. 3, 2011).
http://www.commondreams.org/news/2011/03/10/gulf-spill-sickness-wrecking-lives.

15. Marc Schwartz, Donna Heimiller, Steve Haymes, and Walt Musial, June 2010. *Assessment of Offshore Wind Energy Resources for the United States.* Technical Report NREL/TP-500-45889
Table B9 Louisiana Offshore wind resource. Online: NREL offshore wind potentail45889.pdf.

BP Oil Spill Settlement 2015

16. CNN, "Historic Settlement Reached for BP Oil Spill" (July 7, 2015).
http://www.cnn.com/2015/07/02/politics/historic-settlement-reached-for-bp-oil-spill/.

17. Robert Wood, "BP Does Not Stand for Big Penalty," *Forbes* (July 3, 2017).
http://www.forbes.com/sites/robertwood/2015/07/03/big-oil-spill-tax-write-off-shows-bp-does-not-stand-for-big-penalty/.

Sun Rising Sutra

Civilization and the rise of the machine is classically considered by Lewis Mumford in his *Pentagon of Power, the Myth of the Machine* (New York: Harcourt, Brace, Jovanovich, 1970) and in his earlier *Myth of the Machine: Technics and Human Development* (1966).

In my book *Ecological Democracy* (Boston: South End Press, 1995), I explore the ideology of industrialism that I explore as the still triangle formed by technique, hierarchy, and progress.

Technique as science, technology, and bureaucracy; hierarchy as the order imposed and maintained by power in all its guises; progress as the go code for industrialism where any change in the interest of industrial growth in production, consumption, profit and power is considered the highest good.

The countervailing and healing response of an ecological civilization, a an ecological or green circle, is manifest from the practice of a moral ecology, an awareness of the consequence of all actions; the interconnection and unity of the one and the many, expressed in social terms by the practice of both freedom and community; and the unity of experience and relationship that reflects our sensuous connection to one another and to a living evolving world. (*Ecological Democracy* pp. 161-2). The ecological circle in practice is an expression of the pursuit of sustainability.

Natural Capital

In a world which recognized the inextricable connection between the health of natural capital and the creation of monetary capital, market rules, law, regulations, and corporate charters would mandate and monetize the interconnection between economic growth and ecological improvement. The pursuit of a path leading to pollution, depletion, and ecological damage would be a path of economic ruin. Unfortunately, the current system still makes legal and profitable the creation of free destructive externalities.

Groups such as the Natural Capital Project are attempting to provide economic models as a planning tool that infers value for natural capital as a planning and investment tool.

The complexities discussed below for offshore wind in New England suggest two things to me. First, the need to systematically make changes in market rules and law to make market price and law send clear signals for ecological conduct everywhere. Second, as a transitional step, the requirement to conduct such as a natural capital cost analysis as part of an environmental impact statement is a very useful step.

Natural Capital Project, "Informing Marine Planning in New England," 2014.

http://www.naturalcapitalproject.org/where/newengland.html.

"The Natural Capital Project (NatCap) is providing assistance to several groups in New England in support of marine planning in the region. The waters of the Northeastern U.S. are intensively used for marine transportation, commercial and recreational fisheries, recreational boating, and many others. Recent state and federal emphasis on the development of renewable energy resources—which in the Northeast centers on offshore wind—has accelerated regional interest in strategic planning of existing and anticipated ocean uses. NatCap is working to map and value a range of ecosystem services in the region to ensure that decision makers have scientifically valid information to use for renewable energy siting decisions and for broader marine planning efforts.

A critical component of this engagement to date has been the development of an offshore wind energy model as part of the InVEST software. The model predicts wind power generation, costs, and revenue over space and flexibly incorporates user-specified wind farm designs and economic inputs. Our model and data collection efforts (data tables are distributed with the model) allow for new advances in understanding costs and exploring the net present value (a metric of profitability) of wind farms in various potential locations. In addition, our modeling approach can enhance siting decisions by considering other ocean uses. We are overlaying spatially explicit wind energy value information with maps of other ocean uses to assess likely tradeoffs between user groups and to explore siting opportunities that lead to win-wins. Although the wind energy model was developed to enhance decision making in New England, the InVEST wind energy model comes with worldwide wind energy datasets to ensure its utility in other locations.

Closer to shore, we are examining how coastal habitats protect people and property from sea-level rise and storms. Particularly after hurricane Sandy, there is significant interest in this theme throughout the Northeast and Mid-Atlantic. We are applying the InVEST Coastal Vulnerability model to map where habitats are providing the most protection."

CHAPTER 2.

Climate Change and U.S. Politics

18. Now the End Begins, "13 Similarities Between Obama and Hitler" (2014). http://nowtheendbegins.com/pages/obama/obama-and-hitler-similarities.htm.

19. Ascending Star Seeds, "Fascism in America and the GOP's Right-Wing" (2012). https://ascendingstarseed.wordpress.com/2011/08/12/fascism-in-america-and-the-gops-right-wing/.

British Climate Act

20. Committee on Climate Change, "Carbon Budgets and Targets," Committee on Climate Change, 2015. http://www.theccc.org.uk/tackling-climate-change/reducing-carbon-emissions/carbon-budgets-and-targets/.

Some Republicans Embrace Renewable Energy

21. John Schwartz, "Fissures in GOP as Some Conservatives Embrace Renewable Energy," *NY Times* (Jan 26, 2014). http://www.nytimes.com/2014/01/26/us/politics/fissures-in-gop-as-some-conservatives-embrace-renewable-energy.html?r=0.

Sen. Angus King, ME Introduces Energy Independence Bill

22. Senator Angus King News Room, "King Introduces Bill to Promote Personal Energy Independence," Angus King, United States Senator. May 6, 2015. http://www.king.senate.gov/newsroom/press-releases/king-introduces-bill-to-promote-personal-energy-independence.

Arizona Utility Adds $50 a Month Roof-Top Solar Fee

23. Ari Phillips, "Arizona's New Solar Charge Is 'Unsupportable By Any Economic Analysis,' SolarCity Says," Think Progress, Feb. 27, 2015. http://thinkprogress.org/climate/2015/02/27/3627891/arizona-utility-adds-50-dollar-rooftop-solar-fee/.

Republican Climate Change Attitudes

24. Yale Project on Climate Change Communication, 2015, "Not All Republicans Think Alike on Global Warming," *Yale School of Forestry* (2015). http://environment.yale.edu/climate-communication/article/not-all-republicans-think-alike-about-global-warming/#sthash.rCEtQ7IK.dpuf.

The Breath of Life Sutra

This is a central concern of meditation master Thich Nhat Hanh on returning oneself to the present and inner peace as discussed in his many books. His book *Fear: Essential Wisdom for Getting Through the Storm* (New York: Harper, 2012) was of particular personal resonance for me. http://plumvillage.org/about/thich-nhat-hanh/.

CHAPTER 3.

Freedom and Community in the United States

Sustainability and Gaea Sutra

The coevolution of life and ecosphere and the complexity of its interactions has is transforming the understanding of our relationship to our living planet. The question for the 21st century is that will we move quickly enough to change both our mindset and our behavior to make economic growth and pursuit of profit mean ecological improvement. The existing industrial paradigm is to behave like residents on a timeless hotel earth free to plunder and take advantage of all that can be possessed and transformed from "resources" to product to profit. This, of course, is the path to ecological collapse. The alternative is the appreciation and practice of the coevolutionary model of a living Earth in which our conscious actions are posing grave threats to all life, and in which our conscious pursuit of sustainability is the path toward healing.

An Interesting Interview with Lovelock on Gaea Self-Regulation

25. "James Lovelock, Gaia's Grand Old Man." *Ecology and Environment.* http://environment-ecology.com/gaia/72-james-lovelock-gaia.html

". . . Life clearly does more than adapt to the Earth. It changes the Earth to its own purposes. Evolution is a tightly coupled dance, with life and the material environment as partners. From the dance emerges the entity Gaia . . . I mean that nature favors those organisms which leave the environment in better shape for their progeny to survive."

CHAPTER 4.

Failures of Market Fundamentalism and Climate Change

26. *Sustainability Is Life's Way Sutra*

An interesting examination of linking social and economic for sustainability and ecological resilience is in Fikret Berkes and Carl Folke, 1994. *Linking social and ecological systems for resilience and sustainability.* Beijer International Institute Discussion Series Paper No. 52.
http://dlc.dlib.indiana.edu/dlc/bitstream/handle/10535/4352/Berkes-linking_social_and_ecological_systems_for_resilience_and_sustainability.pdf.

". . . definition of resilience . . . we use here emphasizes conditions in which disturbances (or perturbations) can flip a system from one equilibrium state to another. . . . the important measure of resilience is of the magnitude or scale of disturbance that can be absorbed before the system changes in structure by changing the variables and processes that control behavior. This is the emerging, non-equilibrium, non-linear view of science. Holling's (1986) "science of surprise". . . systems are complex and self-organizing, permeated by uncertainty and discontinuities, as in chaos theory and Pirgogine's irreversible thermodynamic systems (Pirgogine and Stengers, 1984). . . . This kind of science is in many ways sympathetic to "savage thought" of Levi-Strauss (1962) and many indigenous systems of environmental knowledge." (p. 8.)

The Sustainable Adaptability of the Ecosphere

Patrick Blandin, "Ecology and Diversity in the Beginning of the 21st Century: Toward a New Paradigm," *Ecology Revisited: Reflecting on Concepts, Advancing Science.* Edited by Astrid Schwarz and Kurt Jax. (New York: Springer Dordrecht Heidelberg, 2011).
https://books.google.com/books?isbn=9048197449.

Israeli Ecologist Zev Naveh (2000) has held that the "the Total Human Ecosystem is the highest co-evolutionary ecological entity on Earth . . . coevolution makes possible life's sustainability, with new species substituting for others to perform continuously ecological functioning. . . ." p. 212-13.

Zev Naveh, "The Total Human Ecosystem," *BioSceince* 50(4): 357 (2000).

CHAPTER 5.

The Ecological Model and a Circular Economy

Davos Conference on Circular Economy

Ellen MacArthur Foundation, McKinsey & Company, 2014. *Towards the Circular Economy: Accelerating the Scale-Up Across Global Supply Chains* (Geneva: World Economic Forum). Quotes from pages 3 and 10.
http://www3.weforum.org/docs/WEF_ENV_TowardsCircularEconomy_Report_2014.pdf 2015.

A Self-Conscious Symbiont Sutra

27. *Interconnected Mycelium*

Suzzane W. Sinard, "The Foundational Role of Mycorrhizal Networks in Self-Organization of Interior Douglas-Fir Forests," *Forest Ecology and Management,* 258S (2009) S95–S107.
http://www.cof.orst.edu/cof/teach/fs545/Readings/Simard 2009.pdf.

Nick Fleming, "Plants Talk to Each Other Using an Internet of Fungus," BBC.
http://www.bbc.com/earth/story/20141111-plants-have-a-hidden-internet.

CHAPTER 6.

The Venus Project:
A Perfectly Ordered State Without Markets

28. Venus Project, "About the Venus Project (2015)."
https://www.thevenusproject.com/en/about/the-venus-project.

Nexus of Sustainability and Social Practice

29. *See:* United Kingdom, Socialist Group, "Global Warming and Ecological Disasters," Parliamentary Assembly Committee on the Environment, Agriculture and Local and Regional Affairs (2008). Rapporteur: Mr. Alan Meale, United Kingdom, Socialist Group.
http://assembly.coe.int/ASP/Doc/XrefViewHTML.asp?FileID=11800&Language=EN.

"The Assembly considers that the response must be global and based on a shared understanding of the long-term objectives and agreement on the framework for action. This approach should be also applied on a European scale. It urges Council of Europe member states and observer countries to coordinate their action at both European and world level and take account of climate change in their sectoral policies such as spatial planning, water management, land use and agricultural policies, particularly with regard to forestry and the organisation of harvests, so as to counter flood and drought risk."

CHAPTER 7.
The Nexus of Freedom and Community

30. *See*: John Rawls, *A Theory of Justice*, (Cambridge: Harvard University Press, 1971) and John Stewart Mill, *On Liberty*, published in 1859. 2011 edition. Project Gutenberg.
https://www.gutenberg.org/files/34901/34901-h/34901-h.htm.

A Moral Ecology

31. *See:* Tim Dean, "Moral Ecology Defined (At Last),"*Ockham's Beard* (2012).
https://ockhamsbeard.wordpress.com/2012/05/06/moral-ecology/.

"Moral ecology describes the phenomenon whereby it takes a pluralism of behavioral strategies to promote high levels of cooperation within groups, and the complex dynamics of the interactions between these strategies over time. It refers to the fact that each behavioral strategy–which is often manifest in the form of a moral norm–enjoys differential levels of success in terms of promoting cooperation depending on the environment in which it exists, i.e., the other strategies in play around it."

CHAPTER 8.
California Leads

32. Seeking Alpha, "California's New GHG Reduction Target Is a Huge Boon for the Solar Industry," *Seeking Alpha*.
http://seekingalpha.com/article/3121476-californias-new-ghg-reduction-target-is-a-huge-boon-for-the-solar-industry.

33. Vaclav Smil, "A Global Transition to Renewable Energy Will Take Many Decades," *Scientific American* (2013).
http://www.scientificamerican.com/article/a-global-transition-to-renewable-energy-will-take-many-decades/.

34. Solar City, press release: "SolarCity Introduces Affordable New Energy Storage Services Across the U.S.," Solar City (April 15, 2015).
http://www.solarcity.com/newsroom/press/solarcity-introduces-affordable-new-energy-storage-services-across-us.

35. Roy Morrison, "Rising Sun for Electric Cars," *Policy Innovations* (2009).
http://www.policyinnovations.org/ideas/innovations/data/000039/:pf_printable.

36. Roy Morrison, 2009. "Plan for A Renewable Future." *Fairer Globalization.* http://fairerglobalization.blogspot.com/2009/12/plan-for-renewable-future.html.
Posted by Policy Innovations.

37. Solar City, "Solar City Activates Fund to Finance More Than $1 Billion in Commercial Solar Projects with Investment from Credit Suisse" (Solar City April 22, 2015). http://www.solarcity.com/newsroom/press/solarcity-activates-fund-finance-more-1-billion-commercial-solar-projects-investment.

38. California Public Utilities Commission, 2015. "Renewable Auction Mechanism." http://www.cpuc.ca.gov/PUC/energy/Renewables/hot/Renewable+Auction+Mechanism.htm.

39. Adam Browning, "First RAM Projects on Line in California," Vote Solar (2013). http://votesolar.org/2013/04/30/first-ram-projects-on-line-in-california/.

CHAPTER 9.
Solar Energy Threatens Utilities, Not the Poor

40. Richard Schlesinger, "What's a Watt Worth?" *Energy Biz* (Summer 2015), pages 8-9.

41. Don Bishop, "Modernizing the Electric Grid," *Energy Biz* (Summer 2015), pages 23-25.

42. ***Sustainability As Social Force Sutra***
See: the Papal Encyclical *Laudato Si',* such as:

Pope Francis, *Laudato Si': On Care for Our Common Home.* Encyclical Letter (2015). Vatican City: Libreria Editrice Vaticana. http://w2.vatican.va/content/francesco/en/encyclicals/documents/papa-francesco_20150524_enciclica-laudato-si.html.

There are numerous perspectives applicable to sustainability rising as transformative social force. What will happen will be determined in practice.

Carolyn Merchant, *Radical Ecology: The Search for a Livable World* (New York: Routledge, 2005).

Vandava Shiva, *Making Peace with the Planet.* (London: Pluto Press, 2012).

Mark Engler and Paul Engler, 2014. "Can Frances Fox Piven's Theory of Disruptive Power Create the Next Occupy?" *Waging Non-violence.*

http://wagingnonviolence.org/feature/can-frances-fox-pivens-theory-disruptive-power-create-next-occupy/.

Wolfgang Sachs, ed., *The Development Dictionary* (London: Zed Books, 1992).

CHAPTER 10.
Greenhouse Gases: What's Sustainable, Who's Responsible?

43. World Bank, 2015. "CO$_2$ Emissions."
http://data.worldbank.org/indicator/EN.ATM.CO2E.PC.

44. Carbon Dioxide Information Analysis Center, 2015. "2013 Global Carbon Project."
http://cdiac.ornl.gov/GCP/carbonbudget/2013/.

45. Hans-Josef Fell, *Global Cooling: Strategies for Climate Action* (London: R Press, Taylor & Francis Group, 2012).

46. EPA, 2015. "Global Greenhouse Gas Emissions Data."
http://www.epa.gov/climatechange/ghgemissions/global.htm.

47. NOAA Research, 2015. "Trends in Atmospheric Carbon Dioxide." Earth Systems Research Laboratory, National Oceanic and Atmospheric Administration.
http://www.esrl.noaa.gov/gmd/ccgg/trends.

48. Duncan Clark, "Which Nations are Most Responsible for Climate Change? *The Guardian*. April 21, 2011.
http://www.theguardian.com/environment/2011/apr/21/countries-responsible-climate-change.

China: Global Warming Emissions and Renewable Development

49. Yang Li, "Wind Power Capacity Near China Development Target," Xinhua (2014).
http://news.xinhuanet.com/english/china/2014-10/22/c_133734929.

50. Yan, "China adds 3.32 GW of solar capacity in HI," Xinhua (2014).
http://news.xinhuanet.com/english/china/2014-08/08/c_133540443.

51. An, "Carbon Emission Data Not the Whole Story," Xinhua (Sept. 24, 2015).
http://news.xinhuanet.com/english/china/2014-09/24/c_133669546.

52. Fu Peng, "China Approves Plan to Combat Climate Change," Xinhua (2014).
http://news.xinhuanet.com/english/sci/2014-09/19/c_133655788.

53. Yang Li, "Chinese Statisticians Broaden Focus from GDP," Xinhua (1914).
http://news.xinhuanet.com/english/china/2014-09/12/c_133638734.

54. Tang Danlu, "Xinhua Insight: Discovering China's New, Normal Growth" (2014).
http://news.xinhuanet.com/english/indepth/2014-10/03/c_133691531.

55. BBC, 2014. "US and China Leaders in 'Historic' Greenhouse Gas Emissions Pledge." (Nov 12, 2014).
http://www.bbc.com/news/world-asia-china-30015545."

56. Fergus Green and Nicholas Stern, *China's "New Normal": Structural Change, Better Growth, and Peak Emission,* "Grantham Research Institute on Climate Change and the Environment, 2015. Quote p. 6. http://www.lse.ac.uk/GranthamInstitute/wpcontent/uploads/2015/06/Chinas_new_normal_green_stern_June_2015.pdf.

Sustainability As Enchantment, Not Reduction

57. *Epistemology Redefines Ontology*

An ecological civilization by its nature is rooted in the dynamic pursuit of sustainability and the knowledge that the nature of things is rooted in coevolutionary change, albeit at differing paces, and emergence of new phenomena. Therefore, ontology, being recedes as a timeless archetypal archetypal quality and is redefined by epistemology, knowledge, that is participatory, rooted in the interconnection of the one and the many and rooted in the practice of a moral-ecology, an awareness that our actions have consequences.

58. *White Storks Looks Up Qi Gong Pose*

I'm told it resets the autonomic nervous system and helps overcome tension and fear. Standing on one foot, like a crane arms spread and lifted overhead as if they were wings, you become surprisingly stable. I do it in the aisles on long plane flights.

Michael P. Garofalo, "Crane Animal Frolics Qui Gong," *Green Way Research* (2013).
http://www.egreenway.com/qigong/crane.htm.

"The Crane develops balance, lightness and agility.
  The Crane cools and relaxes your whole body, balances the heart-energy, gently stretches your ligaments and releases your spine.
  The Crane exercises strengthen the Heart organ system and benefits the circulation and lungs.
  The Crane must be light and soaring, calm and tranquil. Avoid heaviness and clumsiness.
  The Classic says, "The Crane is graceful, standing like a pine. It opens its wings and soars into the clouds. Spreading its wings, it lands, poised on one leg. Its *qi* rises and sinks with no sense of heaviness.""

CHAPTER 11.
What Can Happen

Paleocene /Eocene Thermal Maximum

59. Appy Sluijs, Mark Pagani, Henk Brinkhuis, Japp S. Sinninghe Damsté, Gerald R. Dickens, Martin Huber, Gert-Jan Reichart, Jens Matthiessen, Ruediger Stein,Lucas J. Lourens, Nikolai Pedentchouk, Jan Backman,

Kathryn Moran, 2006. "Subtropical Arctic Ocean temperatures during the Paleocene/Eocene thermal maximum."*Nature* 441, 610-613 (June 1, 2006).
http://www.nature.com/nature/journal/v441/n7093/full/nature04668.html\l a3.

Lessons from PETM for Today Include:

James Wight, "The Rapid Pulse of PETM CO2 Followed by Rapid Warming Indicates High Climate Sensitivity," *Skeptical Science.* June 7, 2011.
http://www.skepticalscience.com/christy-crock-6-climate-sensitivity.html.

"CO_2 Does Indeed Appear to Have a Long Atmospheric Lifetime," *Skeptical Science.*
http://www.skepticalscience.com/co2-residence-time.htm.

Rob Painting, "Ocean Acidification: Winners and Losers," *Skeptical Science* (June 10, 2011).
http://www.skepticalscience.com/Ocean_acidification_Winners_and_losers.html.

Ocean acidification (of the deep sea at least) can occur even under conditions of CO2 release much slower than today.

Rob Painting, "CO_2 rising ten times faster than petm extinction," *Skeptical Science* (2011).

Online: http://ww.wskepticalscience.com/co2-rising-ten-times-faster-than-petm-extinction.html

Sustainability and Time's One-Way Arrow Sutra

60. *See, for example*: Jacob D. Haqq-misra and Seth D. Baum, "The Sustainability Solution to the Fermi Paradox," JBIS, Vol. 62, pp.47-51.
http://sethbaum.com/ac/2009_FermiParadox.pdf http://sethbaum.com/ac/2009_FermiParadox.pdf.

CHAPTER 12.
Paths to An Ecologically Sustainable Future

61. *See interesting discussion in:*

Jörg Asmussen, "The Social and Ecological Market Economy in the 21st Century," *Policy Network*, 2014.
http://www.policy-network.net/pno_detail.aspx?ID=4716&title=The-social-and-ecological-market-economy-in-the-21st-century

"What are the requirements to be met by an economic model in the 21st century? There is no denying that a market economy is the best system for achieving the optimal allocation of resources—but only if the market is subject to certain restrictions. On the one hand, we have to prevent the market from increasingly splitting society into the "haves" and the "have-nots." On the other hand, considering our planet's limited resources, we have to find a way to ensure that a system geared to growth can be sustained in the long term. Can there be a more worthwhile project, a more progressive project, a more social-democratic project than turning a free market economy (back) into a social and ecological market economy?"

CHAPTER 13.

A Chinese Ecological Path

China Central Committee April 2015 Ecological Blueprint

62. "Opinions of the CPC Central Committee and the State Council on Further Promoting the Development of Ecological Civilization," Communist Party of China Central Committee, 2015.
    Online: http://environmental-partnership.org/wp-content/uploads/download-folder/Eco-Guidelines rev Eng.pdf.

Green Development Bank

63. Stephen Eagle, "Green Bank Proposed in China as Pollution Mounts," *Bloomberg* (2015).
    http://www.bloomberg.com/news/videos/2015-04-23/-green-bank-proposed-in-china-as-pollution-mounts.

Asia Infrastructure and Investment Bank (AIIB)

64. Zhang Chun, "Civil Society Call for China-led Development Bank to Foster Green Growth." *China Dialogue* (2015).
    https://www.chinadialogue.net/blog/7878-Civil-society-call-for-China-led-development-bank-to-foster-green-growth/en.

East Asian SuperGrid

65. Faulkner, Roger, Morrison, Roy, Jennifer Wells, "A China-East Asia Efficient Renewable Supergrid" (2013). China International Working Groups.
    Online: http://www.ciwg.net/files/74235701.pdf http://www.ciwg.net/files/74235701.pdf.

    and

Kyu-won Jeong, Kwang-hee Hong, Sung-yun Hong, Kab-ho Park, Hong-gyun Kim, Bong-soo Moon, Construction the North-East Asian Supergrid for Co-prosperity and Peace. *Cigre,* 2014.
Online: http://www.cigre-thailand.org/tncf/events/aorc2014/full_paper/1076R.pdf.

China's New Normal

66. Fergus Green and Nicholas Stern, "China's 'New Normal': Structural Change, Better Growth, and Eeak Emissions." Grantham Research Institute on climate Change and the Environment, 2015. Quote p. 6. http://www.lse.ac.uk/GranthamInstitute/wpcontent/uploads/2015/06/Chinas_new_normal_green_stern_June_2015.pdf.

CHAPTER 14.
China's Ecological Pivot:
A Report from the World Cultural Forum

67. "The 2nd World Cultural Forum on Ecological Civilization Held in Hangzhou, China in 2013," World Cultural Forum, 2013. Online: http://www.thffc.com/tcf_en/nianhui-list.php page_argu=TCF+Second+Annual+Conference%2C2013&id=2.

68. World Cultural Forum, Hangzhou Declaration, 2013. http://www.ciwg.net/hangzhou-declaration.html.

Ecological Civilization

69. Roy Morrison, *Ecological Democracy* (Boston: South End Press, 1995).

Declaration of Support for an Efficient Renewable Energy Future

70. Dave Andrews, Godfrey Boyle, Gregor Czisch, Mark Delucchi, Mark Z. Jacobson, Nick Jenkins, Daniel Kammen, Roy Morrison, Andrew Smith, Candida Spillard, *Policy Innovations* (July 19, 2010). http://www.policyinnovations.org/ideas/innovations/data/000170.

Advanced Energy Performance Contracting

71. Roy Morrison, "Advanced Energy Performance Contracting" (2013). http://www.ecocivilizationweebly.com/advanced-energy-performance-contracting-1-page-summary.html.

Global Cooling Strategies and Initiatives

72. Hans-Josef Fell, *Global Cooling: Strategies for Climate Protection* (London: CRC Press, Taylor & Francis Group, 2012).

Renewable Energy Hedge Agreements

73. Roy Morrison, "Renewable Energy Hedges," *Policy Innovations* (2008). http://www.policyinnovations.org/ideas/innovations/data/000038.

The Path Sutra

74. For discussion of biological altruism in organisms with complex social structures from bee, ants, bats, monkeys, and humans, see:

Stanford Encyclopedia of Philosophy, 2003. "Biological Altruism." http://plato.stanford.edu/entries/altruism-biological/.

"For example, vampire bats regularly regurgitate blood and donate it to other members of their group who have failed to feed that night, ensuring they do not starve. In numerous bird species, a breeding pair receives help in raising its young from other 'helper' birds, who protect the nest from predators and help to feed the fledglings. Vervet monkeys give alarm calls to warn fellow monkeys of the presence of predators, even though in doing so they attract attention to themselves, increasing their personal chance of being attacked."
See notes on BIG and BEE sections following:

CHAPTER 15.
A BIG and a BEE

Convergence of Biological and Social Evolution Sutra

75. Interesting discussion of biological and social evolution and evolutionary convergence in:
Stephen K. Sanderson, 1999. *Social Transformations: A General Theory of Historical Development.* (Lanham, Maryland: Rowman and Littlefield).

CHAPTER 16.
A BEE

A Basic Income Guarantee (BIG) and a Basic Energy Entitlement (BEE) are examples of two complementary global mechanisms for the global pursuit of both a renewable energy future upon a framework of fairness and social justice. An ecological civilization will not emerge simply by building green machines in a world riven by the intractable misery of billions. Income generated from BEE investments can help fund the BIG. Sustainability and an ecological global growth agenda as a successful global practice is ultimately about the global success of an ecological justice movement that ends both poverty and ecological pillage. This is a recipe for a richer, more interdependent, and more just world.

http://stats.oecd.org/viewhtml.aspx?datasetcode=NAAG_2014&lang=en.

BEE Defined

76. United Nations Department of Economic and Social Affairs (UNDESA), 2011. World Economic and Social Survey 2011—The Great Green Technological Transformation, Chapter 2.

http://www.un.org/en/development/desa/policy/wess/wess_current/2011wess_chapter2.pdf.

OECD National Account Statistics:
Data on Gross Domestic Products at Current Prices

77. OECD, 2015. National Accounts at a Glance 2014. *OECD.stat*. http://stats.oecd.org/viewhtml.aspx?datasetcode=NAAG_2014&lang=en

78. UNDESA, 2011. op.cit. http://www.un.org/en/development/desa/policy/wess/wess_current/2011wess_chapter2.pdf.

Energy Efficiency, Second Law, Carnot Cycle and Carbon

79. Ljubisa R. Radovic, *"Efficiency of Energy Conversion."* Chapter 4 (Penn State College of Earth and Mineral Sciences). http://www.ems.psu.edu/~radovic/Chapter4.pdf.

"Carbon Dioxide Emissions Coefficients," U.S. Energy Information Agency, (2013). http://www.eia.gov/environment/emissions/co2_vol_mass.cfm.

Driving Efficiency

80. "All Electric Vehicles." U.S. Department of Energy (2015). http://www.fueleconomy.gov/feg/evtech.shtml.

Global Energy Outlook and the Poor

81. OECD, 2015. National Accounts at a Glance 2014. *OECD.stat*.

82. International Energy Agency, *World Energy Outlook* (2015). http://www.worldenergyoutlook.org/resources/energydevelopment/.

Solar Lights for Solar Africa Youth

83. Ed Bender, "Solar Empowerment for South African Youth," *Indiegogo* (2015). https://www.indiegogo.com/projects/solar-empowerment-for-south-african-youth#/story

One Million Lights: *see* online: http://onemillionlights.org.

Economic Growth as Ecological Improvement Sutra

84. *See my book*: Roy Morrison, *Markets, Democracy and Survival.* (Warner, New Hampshire: Writers Publishing Cooperative, 2007). www.beechriverbooks.com/id19.html.

CHAPTER 17.
A BIG

85. Andre Gorz, *Critique of Economic Reason* (London: Verso, 1989).
   http://www.versobooks.com/books/509-critique-of-economic-reason

86. ***U.S. B.I.G. Network***

Good place to start for right and left wing perspectives on a BIG:
http://www.usbig.net/

BIEN Basic Income Earth Network

For a European perspective, *see:* http://www.basicincome.org/

Brazil's Bolsa Família

87. ***Alaska Permanent Fundamental Fund***
   Annual Performance Data
   http://www.apfc.org/home/Content/dividend/dividendamounts.cfm.

88. World Bank, 2013, "Bolsa Família: Changing the Lives of Millions in Brazil."
   Online: http://web.worldbank.org/WBSITE/EXTERNAL/NEWS/0,
   contentMDK:21447054~pagePK:64257043~piPK:437376~theSitePK:4607,00.html.

89. Karl Marx, *Manifesto of the Communist Party,* 1848. Chapter one Marx Engels Archive.
   https://www.marxists.org/archive/marx/works/1848/communist-manifesto/ch01.htm.

90. ***Sustainabilty Rising Sutra***

Emergence

Emergence is a pervasive phenomena of scale and complexity, the sudden appearance of new phenomena operating in the world on scales ranging from quantum physics to biological and social systems.

Emergent Phenomena in Quantum Systems:

". . . The Emergent Phenomena in Quantum Systems (EPiQS) Initiative promotes fundamental research on quantum materials, systems in which strong interactions among constituent electrons lead to a great variety of emergent phenomena—cooperative behaviors that cannot be predicted from the properties of individual electrons. The best-known example is high-temperature superconductivity, in which electrons form bound pairs despite their electrical repulsion and flow without any resistance. Other, equally striking, emergent phenomena include: "heavy" electrons that appear to be hundreds or thousands of times more massive than free electrons; exotic "emergent particles" with properties different from any known elementary particle; and electrons that self-organize into complex spatial patterns, reminiscent of the behavior of molecules in a liquid crystal display.

Gordon and Betty Moore Foundation, "Emergent Phenomena in Quantum Systems" (2015).
http://www.moore.org/programs/science/emergent-phenomena-in-quantum-systems.

A good introduction to emergence from the biological realm from New England Complex Systems Institute is this:

Yaneer Bar-Yam, "Concepts: Emergence," New England Complex Systems Institute (2011).
http://necsi.edu/guide/concepts/emergence.html

"Emergence refers to the existence or formation of collective behaviors—what parts of a system do together that they would not do alone.

In describing collective behaviors, emergence refers to how collective properties arise from the properties of parts, how behavior at a larger scale arises from the detailed structure, behavior and relationships at a finer scale. For example, cells that make up a muscle display the emergent property of working together to produce the muscle's overall structure and movement. A water molecule has emergent properties that arise out of the properties of oxygen and hydrogen atoms. Many water molecules together form river flows and ocean waves. Trees, other plants and animals form a forest.

When we think about emergence we are, in our mind's eye, moving among views at different scales. We see the trees and the forest at the same time, in order to see how the trees and the forest are related to each other. We might consider particularly those details of the trees that are important in giving rise to the behavior of the forest.

In conventional views the observer considers either the trees or the forest. Those who consider the trees consider the details to be essential and do not see the patterns that arise when considering trees in the context of the forest. Those who consider the forest do not see the details. When one can shift back and forth between seeing the trees and the forest one also sees which aspects of the trees are relevant to the description of the forest. Understanding this relationship in general is the study of emergence.

In describing *function, emergence suggests that there* are properties that we associate with a system that are actually properties of the relationship between a system and its environment."

CHAPTER 18.

Be Afraid, Be Very Afraid

91. Barack Obama, "Remarks to United Coast Guard Academy Commencement" (May 20, 2015, White House Press Office).
https://www.whitehouse.gov/the-press-office/2015/05/20/remarks-president-united-states-coast-guard-academy-commencement.

Life and Mind Are Coextensive Sutra

92. Gregory Bateson, *Mind and Nature: A Necessary Unity (Advances in Systems Theory, Complexity, and the Human Sciences)* (New York: Hampton Press, 2002).

"But the bits and pieces of mind which appear before consciousness invariably give a false picture of mind as a whole. The systemic character of mind is never there depicted, because the sampling is governed by purpose. We never see in consciousness that the mind is like an ecosystem—a self-corrective network of circuits. We only see arcs of these circuits. And the instinctive vulgarity of scientists consists precisely in mistaking these arcs for the larger truth . . ." p.8.

Gregory Bateson's concepts of mind and cybernetics are of the greatest significance.

CHAPTER 19.

A Twenty-Eighth Amendment to the Constitution

93. Abraham Lincoln, "House Divided," speech given in Springfield, Illinois, June 16, 1858.
http://www.abrahamlincolnonline.org/lincoln/speeches/house.htm.

CHAPTER 20.

Solar Lights for South Africa

94. Sundance Solar, 2015. "Sunbender Do-it-Yourself Solar LED Jar Light Kit-Pre-wired, no soldering."
Online: http://store.sundancesolar.com/sunbender-do-it-yourself-solar-led-jar-light-kit-pre-wired-no-soldering/ This system is being adapted for African student assembly and sale.

95. Angazda Design Pay Go System.
http://www.angazadesign.com.

Sustainability Speaks Sutra

96. William Rees, "What's blocking Sustainability," *Science, Practice, & Policy.* Volume 6, Issue 2 (2010).
    http://whatcom.wsu.edu/carbonmasters/documents/BlockingSustainability Final1010.pdf.

"My working hypothesis is that modern H. sapiens is unsustainable by nature—unsustainability is an inevitable emergent property of the systemic interaction between contemporary technoindustrial society and the ecosphere. I trace this conundrum to humanity's once-adaptive, sub-conscious, genetic predisposition to expand (shared with all other species), a tendency reinforced by the socially constructed economic narrative of continuous material growth. Unfortunately,these qualities have become maladaptive. The current coevolutionary pathway of the human enterprise and the ecosphere therefore puts civilization at risk—both defective genes and malicious "memes" can be "selected out" by a changing physical environment. To achieve sustainability, the world community must write a new cultural narrative that is explicitly designed for living on a finite planet, a narrative that overrides humanity's outdated innate expansionist tendencies."

CHAPTER 21.
Ecological Tax Transformation

European Eco Taxes

97. International Labour Organization, *The Double Dividend and Environmental Tax Reforms in the European Union*
    http://www.ilo.org/public/english/bureau/inst/research/ecinst/dp13.pdf.

CHAPTER 22.
Assessments on Pollution, Depletion, and Ecological Damage

98. Roy Morrison, *Markets, Democracy and Survival.* (Warner, New Hampshire: Writers Publishing Cooperative, 2007).

99. *Brazil Ecological Taxation*

Anna Mey Marmo, "Green Taxation," World Resources Institute
http://www.wri.org/blog/2009/11/green-taxation.

100. *See:* John Quiggin, "Discount Rates and Sustainability," *International Journal of Social Economics* (1997).
     http://www.uq.edu.au/economics/johnquiggin/JournalArticles97/ Sustain97.pdf.

"A policy which generated substantial increases in consumption in the short term, but degraded resources to such an extent that living standards declined continuously in the future could easily be found to be beneficial using standard discounting procedures."

CHAPTER 23.
China and Potential for Ecological Value–Added Taxes

101. Xu Yan, *"China's VAT Experience."* TaxAnalysis.com (2011), p.322. http://www.taxanalysts.com/www/freefiles.nsf/Files/YAN-25.pdf/$-file/YAN-25.pdf.

102. National Bureau of Statics of China, "China Statistical Yearbook 2009: 7-2 Taxes," http://www.stats.gov.cn/tjsj/ndsj/2009/indexch.htm.

103. Zhang Chun, "China Issues Draft on Environmental Taxes to Combat Pollution," China Dialogue. https://www.chinadialogue.net/article/show/single/en/7975-China-issues-draft-on-environmental-taxes-to-combat-pollution.

104. *Sustainability and the Biosphere's System State*

For a discussion of ecological ethics and sustainability, *see:*
Tim Madigan, "Ecological Ethics," *Philosophy Now.* (Apr/May 2015). https://philosophynow.org/issues/88/Ecological_Ethics.

"Dewey attempted to break down dualisms which led to antagonisms and misunderstandings. Perhaps 'biocentrism' and 'anthropocentrism' are such dualisms. If species are both interacting and constantly evolving, then our speciesism is indeed problematic. Dewey's call for an evolutionary ethical approach is still a worthy cause, and one which can give philosophical support to the continuing efforts to implement sustainability. Contemplating the possibility of the end of the human species or human civilization is a necessary step, but is not an ethically acceptable end to aim for. As another noted pragmatist, Benjamin Franklin, put it in a different context: we must all hang together, or assuredly we will all hang separately."

CHAPTER 24.
India: The Renewable Energy Imperative

105. Wikipedia, "States of India by Installed Power Capacity" (2015). http://en.wikipedia.org/wiki/States_of_India_by_installed_power_capacity

106. Aman Shah, Clara Ferreira-Marques, and Ruth Pitchford, "SunEdison, Adani to invest $4 billion in Indian solar panel plant." Reuters (2015). Online:

http://in.reuters.com/article/2015/01/11/india-solar-sunedison
-idINKBN0KK0M420150111.

CHAPTER 25.
Bangladesh: Problems and Opportunities

107. World Bank, 2013, "Warming Climate to Hit Bangladesh Hard with
Sea Level Rise, More Floods and Cyclones, World Bank Report Says."
http://www.worldbank.org/en/news/press-release/2013/06/19/warming-
climate-to-hit-bangladesh-hard-with-sea-level-rise-more-floods-and-
cyclones-world-bank-report-says.

108. Bidisha Banjerjee, "India Is Fencing Off Its Border with Bangladesh.
What Will That Mean for Millions of Potential Climate Refugees?"
Slate (2013).
http://www.slate.com/authors.bidisha_banerjee.html.

109. Grammen Shakti Large Scale Grassroots Solar. See their website on Solar
Home Systems:
http://www.gshakti.org/index.php?option=com_content&view=
article&id=58&Itemid=62

110. For recent wind developments *see* Siemens, "Siemens highlights cost-
cutting innovations for offshore wind at European trade show Hamburg"
(Feb. 26, 2015).
http://www.siemens.com/press/en/pressrelease/press=/en/pressrelease/
2015/windpowerrenewables/pr2015020140wpen.htm&content[]=
WP&content[]=EM.

New advancements in wind turbine technology

Major breakthrough in reducing grid access costs

Innovative offshore logistics concepts for turbine maintenance

111. First Solar, "Utility Scale Generation" (2015).
http://www.firstsolar.com/en/solutions/utility-scale-generation.

112. "Bangladesh and Coal," Source Watch Org.
http://www.sourcewatch.org/index.php/Bangladesh_and_coal.

113. Channel News Asia, 2015. "India Firms to Sign Giant Power Deals with
Bangladesh."
http://www.channelnewsasia.com/news/asiapacific/india-firms-to-
sign-giant/1895786.html

"Top Indian Conglomerates Reliance and Adani Plan to Invest Billions of
Dollars in Bangladesh's Rickety Power Sector, officials announced Friday
(June 5) on the eve of a visit to Dhaka by Prime Minister Narendra Modi."

114. ***Sustainability as an Emergent Property of Ecosphere Sutra***

See: Michael P. Weinstein, R. Eugene Turner, & Carles Ibáñez," The Global Sustainability Transition: It Is More Than Changing Light Bulbs," *Sustainability, Practice & Politics* (2013).
http://sspp.proquest.com/archives/vol9iss1/1203-005.weinstein.html.

CHAPTER 26.

Bangladesh and Louisiana: A Cautionary Tale

115. "New Orleans' Lower Ninth Ward Targeted for Gentrification" *The Guardian* (2015).
http://www.theguardian.com/us-news/2015/jan/23/new-orleans-lower-ninth-ward-condos-gentrification.

116. ***The Garden of Life Sutra***

See: Stephen Ponder, "Coevolution of life and landscapes." *Proceedings of National Academy of Sciences.* Vol. 111 No. 9 (2014), p. 3207-8.

"(1). As our understanding of biogeochemistry, weathering, and geomorphology has grown, so have our observations of life's imprint on earth's surface morphology. It has been proposed that even plate tectonics (2) and the rise of continents (3) may be linked to the presence of life. Just as the land is shaped by life, life is shaped by the landscapes it inhabits (4). Geologic contacts often underlie ecological boundaries (5), and surface geology in soil-mantled landscapes is commonly inferred from the distribution of vegetation. In PNAS, Hahm et al. (6) provide an elegant illustration of the two-way interaction between the evolution of life and land."

CHAPTER 27.

Global Tour: Places Working to Get It Right

117. ***California Utilities to Spend $1 Billion on Electric Car Charging Stations***

Herman K. Trabish, "Co-op offers renewables only EV charging, highlighting new opportunity for utilities:Selling off-peak renewable kWhs to beat the rising cost of gasoline could also drive an EV boom," *Utility Dive* (2015).
Online: http://www.utilitydive.com/news/co-op-offers-renewables-only-ev-charging-highlighting-new-opportunity-for/400779.

Jonathan Marsh, "PG&E Leads the Nation in Offering Electric Vehicle Rates." *Currents PG&E* (2014).
http://www.pgecurrents.com/2014/07/29/pge-leads-the-nation-in-offering-electric-vehicle-rates/.

PG&E PLUG in EV Calculator

EV's calculator is online.
See: http://www.pge.com/cgi-bin/pevcalculator/PEV.

Monthly EVs Sales Scorecard

"Monthly Plug-In Sales Scorecard," Inside EVs, 2015.
http://insideevs.com/monthly-plug-in-sales-scorecard.

118. Jonathan Marsh, "PG&E Leads the Nation in Offering Electric Vehicle Rates." *Currents PG&E* (2014).
http://www.pgecurrents.com/2014/07/29/pge-leads-the-nation-in-offering-electric-vehicle-rates/.

Monthly EVs Sales Scorecard

"Monthly Plug-In Sales Scorecard," Inside EVs, 2015.
Online: http://insideevs.com/monthly-plug-in-sales-scorecard/.

119. Herman K.Trabish, "New Vermont Law Mandates 75% Renewables by 2032, Targets Residential Emissions." *Utility Dive* (2015).
Online: http://www.utilitydive.com/news/new-vermont-law-mandates-75-renewables-by-2032-targets-residential-emissi/400777/.

120. Vermont Public Service Dept. 2014. *Total Energy Study. Vt Public Service Dept.* Montpelier, VT.
http://publicservice.vermont.gov/sites/psd/files/Pubs_Plans_Reports/TES/TES%20FINAL%20Report%2020141208.pdf.

121. Jake Richardson, "100% Renewable Energy Goal For Hawaii: Governor Signs Bill" (2015).
http://www.pge.com/cgi-bin/pevcalculator/PEV

122. Susan Kraemer, "Competitive Without Subsidies: Navigating the Booming Solar Market in Chile." *PV Insider* (2014). Online:
http://analysis.pv-insider.com/industry-insight/competitive-without-subsidies-navigating-booming-solar-market-chile

123. World Future Council, 2015. "Japan's Top Runner Programme," Future Policy.org.
http://www.futurepolicy.org/ecologically-intelligent-design/japans-top-runner-programme/

124. "Carbon Emissions from Peat Lands," Wetlands.org., Wetlands International, 2015.
http://www.wetlands.org/Whatarewetlands/Peatlands/Carbonemissionsfrompeatlands/tabid/2738/Default.aspx.

125. Kemen Austin, Ariana Alisjahbana, Andika Putraditama, Fred Stolle, Taryono Darusman, Rachmat Boediono, Bambang Eko Budianto,

Christian Purba, Giorgio Budi Indrarto and Erica Pohnan, *Indonesia's Forest Moratorium: Impacts and Next Steps* (2014). World Resource Institute. http://www.wri.org/publication/indonesias-forest-moratorium.

126. Sapariah Saturi, Ridzki Ridzki Sigit, Indra Nugraha and Philip Jacobson, "Indonesia extends moratorium on partial forest clearing." *Guardian: Mongabay Environmental Network* 2015).
http://www.theguardian.com/environment/2015/may/14/indonesia-extends-moratorium-on-partial-forest-clearing.

127. Stu Robarts, "AeroFarms to Open 'World's Largest Indoor Vertical Farm,'" *GizMag* (2015). Online:
http://www.gizmag.com/aerofarm-indoor-vertical-farm/38380/.

128. State of Green, "Profile: City of Copenhagen" (2015).
https://stateofgreen.com/en/profiles/city of-copenhagen.

129. Danish Architecture Center, "Copenhagen: Sustainability at District Plan Level."
http://www.dac.dk/en/dac-cities/sustainable-cities/all-cases/master-plan/copenhagen-sustainability-at-district-plan-level/.

130. ***Sustainability in the 21st Sutra***

Sustainability As Summary Equations of Eco-System State

See Roy Morrison, "The New Science of Sustainable Dynamics." *Policy Innovations* (Dec. 18, 2008).
http://www.policyinnovations.org/ideas/innovations/data/000081.

"The challenge of self-consciousness in the twenty-first century, and of sustainability as a science and practice, is to understand and respond to the consequences of human action on a planetary scale. Sustainability is a science of dynamic equilibrium and of change, addressing actions that are local and global, and consequences that can be both immediate and influential over geologic periods of time."

References

Aman Shah, Clara Ferreira-Marques, and Ruth Pitchford, "SunEdison, Adani to Invest $4 Billion In Indian Solar Panel Plant," Reuters (2015). http://in.reuters.com/article/2015/01/11/india-solar-sunedison-idINKBN0KK0M420150111.

"Carbon Emission Data Not the Whole Story," Xinhua (Sept. 24, 2015). http://news.xinhuanet.com/english/china/2014-09/24/c_133669546.

Dave Andrews, Godfrey Boyle, Gregor Czisch, Mark Delucchi, Mark Z. Jacobson, Nick Jenkins, Daniel Kammen, Roy Morrison, Andrew Smith, Candida Spillard, *Policy Innovations* (July 19, 2010). http://www.policyinnovations.org/ideas/innovations/data/000170

"Fascism in America and the GOP's Right-Wing," Ascending Star Seed, 2012. https://ascendingstarseed.wordpress.com/2011/08/12/fascism-in-america-and-the-gops-right-wing/

Asian Development Bank. 39653-023: MFF: Guangdong Energy Efficiency and Environment Improvement Investment Program, Tranche 1. http://www.adb.org/projects/39653-023/details.

Jörg Asmussen, "The Social and Ecological Market Economy in the 21st Century," *Policy Network* (2014). http://www.policy-network.net/pno_detail.aspx?ID=4716&title=The-social-and-ecological-market-economy-in-the-21st-century.

Kemen Austin, Ariana Alisjahbana, Andika Putraditama, Fred Stolle, Taryono Darusman, Rachmat Boediono, Bambang Eko Budianto, Christian Purba, Giorgio Budi Indrarto and Erica Pohnan, *Indonesia's Forest Moratorium: Impacts and Next Steps*. World Resource Institute (2014). http://www.wri.org/publication/indonesias-forest-moratorium.

Bidisha Banerjee, "India Is Fencing Off Its Border with Bangladesh. What Will That Mean for Millions of Potential Climate Refugees?" *Slate* (June 19, 2013). http://www.slate.com/authors.bidisha_banerjee.html. http://www.slate.com/articles/health_and_science/green_room/2010/12/the_great_wallof_india.html.

Gregory Bateson, *Mind and Nature: A Necessary Unity,* Advances in Systems Theory, Complexity, and the Human Sciences (New York: Hampton Press, 2002).

BBC, "US and China Leaders in 'Historic' Greenhouse Gas Emissions Pledge," Nov 12, 2014.
http://www.bbc.com/news/world-asia-china-30015545.

Fikret Berkes and Carl Folke, "Linking Social and Ecological Systems for Resilience and Sustainability," Beijer International Institute Discussion Series Paper No. 52. 1 (1994).
http://dlc.dlib.indiana.edu/dlc/bitstream/handle/10535/4352/Berkes-linking_social_and_ecological_systems_for_resilience_and_sustainability.pdf.

Patrick Blandin, "Ecology and Diversity in the Beginning of the 21st Century: Toward a New Paradigm" in *Ecology Revisited: Reflecting on Concepts, Advancing Science.* Edited by Astrid Schwarz, Kurt Jax (New York: Springer Dordrecht Heidelberg, 2011).
https://books.google.com/books?isbn=9048197449.

Cécile Brugère, *Global Aquaculture Outlook In the Next Decades: An Analysis Of National Aquaculture Production Forecasts to 2030.* (Rome: FAO Fisheries Department, 2004).

Don Bishop, "Modernizing the Electric Grid." *Energy Biz.* Summer 2015.

Adam Browning, "First RAM Projects Online in California," Vote Solar (2013).
http://votesolar.org/2013/04/30/first-ram-projects-on-line-in-california/.

Jason Burke, "India and Bangladesh Seal Border Deal, Four Decades later" (2015).
http://www.theguardian.com/world/2015/jun/06/india-bangladesh-seal-border-territories-deal-mido-hasina.

"Renewable Auction Mechanism," California Public Utilities Commission, 2015.
http://www.cpuc.ca.gov/PUC/energy/Renewables/hot/Renewable+Auction+Mechanism.htm.

Channel News Asia, 2015. "India Firms to Sign Giant Power Deals with Bangladesh."
http://www.channelnewsasia.com/news/asiapacific/india-firms-to-sign-giant/1895786.html.

Meg Cichon, "The Deal: European Supergrid Sets High Expectations," Renewable Energy World.com. Aug. 12, 2012. http://renewableenergyworld.com/rea/news/article/2012/08/the-deal-europeansupergrid-sets-high-expectations.

Carbon Dioxide Information Analysis Center, 2015. "2013 Global Carbon Project." http://cdiac.ornl.gov/GCP/carbonbudget/2013/.

"Historic Settlement Reached for BP Oil Spill," CNN, July7, 2015. http://www.cnn.com/2015/07/02/politics/historic-settlement-reached-for-bp-oil-spill/.

Committee on Climate Change, *"Carbon Budgets and Targets,"* Committee on Climate Change, 2011. http://www.theccc.org.uk/tackling-climate-change/reducing-carbon-emissions/carbon-budgets-and-targets/.

Dahr Jamil, "Gulf Oil Sickness Wrecking Lives," Al Jazeera, March 11, 2011, viewed on Common Dreams.org website. http://www.commondreams.org/news/2011/03/10/gulf-spill-sickness-wrecking-lives.

Communist Party of China Central Committee, 2015. *Opinions of the CPC Central Committee and the State Council on Further Promoting the Development of Ecological Civilization,* 2015. http://environmental-partnership.org/wp-content/uploads/download-folder/Eco Guidelines_rev_Eng.pdf.

Gregor Czisch, 2011. *Scenarios for a Future Electricity Supply: Cost-Optimized Variation on Supplying Europe and its Neighbours with Electricity from Renewable Energies.* Trans. HD editions from the German (London: The Institution of Engineering and Technology).

Department of Energy, 2015. "All Electric Vehicles." U.S. Department of Energy. http://www.fueleconomy.gov/feg/evtech.shtml.

Danish Architecture Center, 2015. "Copenhagen: Sustainability at District Plan Level." Online: http://www.dac.dk/en/dac-cities/sustainable-cities/all-cases/master-plan/copenhagen-sustainability-at-district-plan-level/.

Tim Dean, 2012. "Moral Ecology Defined (At Last),"*Ockham's Beard* (2012). https://ockhamsbeard.wordpress.com/2012/05/06/moral-ecology/.

Jared Diamond, *Collapse: How Societies Choose to Fail or Succeed* (New York: Viking Press, 2005).

Stephen Eagle, "Green Bank Proposed in China as Pollution Mounts," Bloomberg (2015).
http://www.bloomberg.com/news/videos/2015-04-23/-green-bank-proposed-in-china-as-pollution-mounts.

Mark Engler and Paul Engler, "Can Frances Fox Piven's Theory of Disruptive Power Create the Next Occupy? Waging Nonviolence.org (2014). http://wagingnonviolence.org/feature/can-frances-fox-pivens-theory-disruptive-power-create-next-occupy/.

Ecology and Environment, "James Lovelock: Ecology's Grand Old Man," *Ecology and Environment* (2014).
http://environment-ecology.com/gaia/72-james-lovelock-gaia.html.

Efficiency Vermont, 2012. Efficiency Vermont Annual Plan.
http://www.efficiencyvermont.org/docs/about_efficiency_vermont/annual_plans/EVT_AnnualPlan2012.pdf.

Roger Faulkner, Roy Morrison, and Jennifer Wells, "A China-East Asia Efficient Renewable Supergrid," China International Working Groups (2013). http://www.ciwg.net/files/74235701.pdf.

Hans-Josef Fell, *Global Cooling: Strategies for Climate Protection* (London: CRC Press, Taylor & Francis Group, 2012).

Nick Fleming, "Plants Talk to Each Other Using an Internet of Fungus." BBC.
http://www.bbc.com/earth/story/20141111-plants-have-a-hidden-internet.

Steve Friess, "Inside Suburu's Zero Waste Factory," *Take Part*.
http://www.takepart.com/article/2013/12/30/inside-subarus-zero-waste-factory.

Fu Peng, "China Approves Plan to Combat Climate Change," Xinhua.
http://news.xinhuanet.com/english/sci/2014-09/19/c_133655788.

Jacob D. Haqq-misra and Seth D. Baum, "The sustainability solution to the fermi paradox," (JBIS, Vol. 62, 2009) pp.47-51.
http://sethbaum.com/ac/2009_FermiParadox.pdf"

Fergus Green and Nicholas Stern 2015. *China's "new normal":structural change, better growth, and peak emissions.*Grantham Research Institute on climate Change and the Environment. Quote p. 6.
http://www.lse.ac.uk/GranthamInstitute/wpcontent/uploads/2015/06/Chinas_new_normal_green_stern_June_2015.pdf.

First Solar, 2015. "Utility Scale Generation."
http://www.firstsolar.com/en/solutions/utility-scale-generation.

Justin Glls, 2014."*Solar and Wind Alter German Landscape Leaving utilities behind.*" (*New York Times* Sept.14, 2014).

Jennifer Goodman, "Lennar Launches No-Cost Solar Program," *Builder* (2014). Online:
http://www.builderonline.com/building/building-science/lennar-launches-no-cost-solar-program_oy.

"Monthly Plug-In Sales Scorecard," Inside EVs, 2015.
http://insideevs.com/monthly-plug-in-sales-scorecard/

Michael P. Garofalo, 2013. "Crane Animal Frolics Qui Gong," *Green Way Research*. http://www.egreenway.com/qigong/crane.htm.

Gobitec Initiative, 2012.
http://www.gobitec.org/index.php?option=com_content&view=article&id=46&Itemid=34.

Jennifer Goodman, 2014. "Lennar Launches No-Cost Solar Program," *Builder*. http://www.builderonline.com/building/building-science/lennar-launches-no-cost-solar-program_o.

Andre Gorz, *Ecology as Politics* (Boston: SouthEnd Press, 1979).

Andre Gorz, *Critique of Economic Reason* (London: Verso, 1989).

T.E. Graedel and Braden R. Allenby, *Industrial Ecology and Sustainable Engineering.* (Upper Saddle River, NJ: Prentice Hall, 2010).

Jeremy Grantham, 2012. "Welcome to Distopia! Entering a Long Term and Politically Dangerous Food Crisis." GMO Capital Quarterly Letter. July 2012
http://www.scribd.com/doc/101734798/GMOQ2Lettern-Jeremy-Grantham-Welcome-to-Dystopia.

Mark Gorgolewski, Vera Straka, Jordan Edmonds, and Carmela Sergio 2006. *Reuse &* "Recycling of Structural Steel in The Construction & Demolition Process, Final Report 20, March 2006. Department of Architectural Science Faculty of Engineering and Applied Science.
http://www.reuse-steel.org/files/General/Reuse%20steel%20final%20report%20submitted.pdf.

Hangzhou Declaration, 2013.
http://www.ciwg.net/hangzhou-declaration.html.

Hansen, Eric, Rajat Panwar, Richard Vlosky, editors, *The Global Forest Sector: Changes, Practices, and Prospect* (Boca Raton, Florida: CRC Press, Taylor and Francis Group, 2013).

Edgar G. Hertwich and Glen P. Peters, 2009. "Carbon Footprint of Nations: A Global, Trade-Linked Analysis." Industrial Ecology Programme and Department of Energy and Process Engineering.

The Guardian, "New Orleans' Lower Ninth Ward Targeted for Gentrification" (2015).
http://www.theguardian.com/us-news/2015/jan/23/new-orleans-lower-ninth-ward-condos-gentrification

International Energy Agency, 2015. *World Energy Outlook.*
http://www.worldenergyoutlook.org/resources/energydevelopment/.

International Labour Organization, *The Double Dividend And Environmental Tax Reforms In The European Union.*
http://www.ilo.org/public/english/bureau/inst/research/ecinst/dp13.pdf.

Senator Angus King News Room, "King Introduces Bill to Promote Personal Energy Independence," Angus King United States Senator, May 6, 2015.
http://www.king.senate.gov/newsroom/press-releases/king-introduces-bill-to-promote-personal-energy-independence.

Martin Luther King Jr, "Beyond Vietnam." Speech April 4, 1967, N.Y., New York.
http://mlk-kpp01.stanford.edu/index.php/encyclopedia/documentsentry/doc_beyond_vietnam/.
Viewed Feb. 14, 2015.

Claire Kreycik, Toby D. Couture, Karlynn S. Cory, 2011. *Innovative Feed-In Tariff Designs that Limit Policy Costs,* National Renewable Energy Laboratory. Golden Colorado. pp. 29-30.
http://www.nrel.gov/docs/fy11osti/50225.pdf.

Kyu-won Jeong, Kwang-hee Hong, Sung-yun Hong, Kab-ho Park, Hong-gyun Kim, Bong-soo Moon, 2014.1 Construction the North-East Asian SuperGrid for Co-prosperity and Peace. Cigre.
http://www.cigre-thailand.org/tncf/events/aorc2014/full_paper/1076R.pdf.

Susan Kraemer, "Competitive Without Subsidies: Navigating the Booming Solar Market in Chile." PV Insider, 2014.
http://analysis.pv-insider.com/industry-insight/competitive-without-subsidies-navigating-booming-solar-market-chile.

John Landers, "China Implements a National Feed in Tariff Rate," August 12, 2011, EnergyTrend.com.
http://www.energytrend.com/China_FIT_08122011.

Karl-Freidrich Lenz, 2012. *Energy from the Mongolian Gobi Desert.*
http://k.lenz.name/LB/wp-content/uploads/2012/04/Lenz-Energy-from-the-Mongolian-Gobi-Desert1.pdf.

Abraham Lincoln, 1858. House Divided speech, Springfield, Illinois (June 16, 1858).
http://www.abrahamlincolnonline.org/lincoln/speeches/house.htm.

Jon Li, "China's Energy Conservation Industry Will Accelerate Its Development in Five Years (2011)" International Energy conservation Environmental Protection Association.
http://www.ieepa.us/news/html/20120713112732.html.

Coco Liu, "China's Energy Saving Service Sector is on the Rise. Energy Efficiency News Net. July 23, 2012.
http://www.eenews.net/public/climatewire/2012/07/23/1.

Amory Lovins, "The Negawatt Revolution: Solving the CO_2 Problem, Keynote Address by Amory Lovinsat, The Green Energy Conference (Montreal 1989). http://www.ccnr.org/amory.html.

Ellen MacArthur Foundation, McKinsey & Company, 2014. *Towards the Circular Economy: Accelerating the Scale-Up Across Global Supply Chains* (Geneva: World Economic Forum). Quote from pages 3 & 10.
http://www3.weforum.org/docs/WEF_ENV_TowardsCircularEconomy_Report_2014.pdf 2015.

Anna Mey Marmo, 2009. "Green Taxation." World Resources Institute. Online: http://www.wri.org/blog/2009/11/green-taxation.

Tim Madigan, "Ecological Ethics," Philosophy Now. Apr/May 2015.
https://philosophynow.org/issues/88/Ecological_Ethics.

Jonathan Marsh, "PG&E Leads the Nation in Offering Electric Vehicle Rates." *Currents PG&E* (2014).
http://www.pgecurrents.com/2014/07/29/pge-leads-the-nation-in-offering-electric-vehicle-rates/.

Karl Marx, 1845. *Manifesto of the Communist Party.* Chapter one Marx Engels Archive.
https://www.marxists.org/archive/marx/works/1848/communist-manifesto/ch01.htm.

Carolyn Merchant, *Radical Ecology: The Search for a Livable World* (New York: Routledge, 2005).

McGill University, 2011. "Feeding the World While Protecting the Planet."
http://www.mcgill.ca/channels/news/feeding-world-while-protecting-planet-202006.

John Stewart Mill, 1859. *On Liberty.* 2011 edition. Project Gutenberg.
https://www.gutenberg.org/files/34901/34901-h/34901-h.htm.

Mongolian Economic Forum, 2012. "Mongolian Renewable Energy."
http://meforum.mn/#!/<>=3>;K=-AM@3MM34ME-M@G8.

Gordon and Betty Moore Foundation, 2015. "Emergent Phenomena in Quantum Systems."
http://www.moore.org/programs/science/emergent-phenomena-in-quantum-systems.

Roy Morrison, *Ecological Democracy* (Boston: South End Press, 1995).

Roy Morrison, *Markets Democracy and Survival* (Warner, New Hampshire: Writers Publishing Cooperative, 2007).

Roy Morrison, "The New Science of Sustainable Dynamics," *Policy Innovations* (2008).
http://www.policyinnovations.org/ideas/innovations/data/000081.

Roy Morrison, "Renewable Energy Hedges," *Policy Innovations* (2008).
http://www.policyinnovations.org/ideas/innovations/data/000038.

Roy Morrison, "Rising Sun for Electric Cars," *Policy Innovations* (2008).
http://www.policyinnovations.org/ideas/innovations/data/000039/:pf_printable.

Roy Morrison, "Plan for A Renewable Future." *Fairer Globalization* (2009).
http://fairerglobalization.blogspot.com/2009/12/plan-for-renewable-future.

Roy Morrison, 2012. "Building an Efficient Renewable Energy System: Advanced Energy performance Contracting as Key Tool."
http://www.ecocivilizationweebly.com/competitively-bid-feed-in-tariff.html.

Lewis Mumford, *Myth of the Machine: Technics and Human Development* (New York: Harcourt, Brace, Jovanovich, 1970, and in his earlier work, 1966).

Lewis Mumford, *Pentagon of Power, the Myth of the Machine* (New York: Harcourt, Brace, Jovanovich, 1970).

Mike Munsell, "Solar PV Pricing Continues to Fall During a Record-Breaking 2014," *Green Tech Media*, 2015.
http://www.greentechmedia.com/articles/read/solar-pv-system-prices-continue-to-fall-during-a-record-breaking-2014.

Zev Naveh, "The Total HumanEcosystem," *BioSceince* 50(4): 357 (2000).

Now the End Begins, "13 Similarities Between Obama and Hitler (2014)" http://nowtheendbegins.com/pages/obama/obama-and-hitler-similarities.htm.

National Bureau of Statics of China, "China Statistical Yearbook 2009: 7-2 Taxes," http://www.stats.gov.cn/tjsj/ndsj/2009/indexch.htm.

Natural CapitalProject, 2014. "Informing Marine Planning in New England," Natural Capital Project.
http://www.naturalcapitalproject.org/where/newengland.html.

NOAA Research, 2015, "Trends in Atmospheric Carbon Dioxide," Earth Systems Research Laboratory, National Oceanic and Atmospheric Administration. http://www.esrl.noaa.gov/gmd/ccgg/trends/

Norwegian University of Science and Technology, 7491 Trondheim, Norway, and Center for International Climate and Environment Research Oslo, P.O. Box. 1129, Blindern, N-0318 Oslo, Norway.
http://pubs.acs.org/doi/pdf/10.1021/es803496a.

OECD, 2015. National Accounts at a Glance 2014. *OECD.stat.*
http://stats.oecd.org/viewhtml.aspx?datasetcode=NAAG_2014&lang=en.

Barack Obama, "Remarks to United Coast Guard Academy Commencement," May 20, 2015. White House Press Office.
https://www.whitehouse.gov/the-press-office/2015/05/20/remarks-president-united-states-coast-guard-academy-commencement.

Rob Painting, "Ocean Acidification: Winners and Losers," *Skeptical Science* (June 10, 2011).
http://www.skepticalscience.com/Ocean_acidification_Winners_and_losers.html.

Rob Painting, "Co2 Rising Ten Times Faster Than Petm Extinction," *Skeptical Science.* Online: http://ww.wskepticalscience.com/co2-rising-ten-times-faster-than-petm-extinction.html.

Ari Phillips, "Arizona's New Solar Charge Is 'Unsupportable by Any Economic Analysis,' SolarCity Says," Think Progress. Feb.27, 2015. http://thinkprogress.org/climate/2015/02/27/3627891/arizona-utility-adds-50-dollar-rooftop-solar-fee/

Stephen Ponder, "Coevolution of Life and Landscapes," *Proceedings of National Academy of Sciences. V*ol. 111 No. 9 (2014), p. 3207-8.

John Quiggin, "Discount Rates and Sustainability," *International Journal of Social Economics* (1997). http://www.uq.edu.au/economics/johnquiggin/JournalArticles97/Sustain97.pdfbg.

Ljubisa R. Radovic (undated). Chapt. 4, *"Efficiency of Energy Conversion.* Penn State College of Earth and Mineral Sciences. http://www.ems.psu.edu/~radovic/Chapter4.pdf.

John Rawls, *A Theory of Justice* (Cambridge: Harvard University Press, 1971).

William Rees, "What's blocking Sustainability," *Science, Practice, & Policy,* Volume 6, Issue 2 (2010). http://whatcom.wsu.edu/carbonmasters/documents/BlockingSustainabilityFinal1010.pdf.

Jake Richardson, "100% Renewable Energy Goal For Hawaii: Governor Signs Bill" (2015). http://www.pge.com/cgi-bin/pevcalculator/PEV.

Stu Robarts, "AeroFarms to Open 'World's Largest Indoor Vertical Farm,'" *GizMag* (2015). http://www.gizmag.com/aerofarm-indoor-vertical-farm/38380/ Wolfgang Sachs, "One World," in

Development Dictionary: A Guide to Knowledge as Power. Ed. by Wolfgang Sachs (London: Zed Books 1992), p. 113.

Stephen K. Sanderson, *Social Transformations: A General Theory of Historical Development.* (Lanham, Maryland: Rowman and Littlefield, 1999).

Sapariah Saturi, Ridzki Ridzki Sigit, Indra Nugraha and Philip Jacobson, 2015. "Indonesia extends moratorium on partial forest clearing." *Guardian: Mongabay Environmental Network*. Online: http://www.theguardian.com/environment/2015/may/14/indonesia-extends-moratorium-on-partial-forest-clearing.

Marc Schwartz, Donna Heimiller, Steve Haymes, and Walt Musial, *Assessment of Offshore Wind Energy Resources for the United States* (June 2010). Technical Report NREL/TP-500-45889 Table B9 Louisiana Offshore wind resource.
Online: NREL offshore wind potentail45889.pdf.

John Schwartz, "Fissures in GOP as Some Conservatives Embrace Renewable Energy," *New York Times*, Jan. 26. 2014. Online: http://www.nytimes.com/2014/01/26/us/politics/fissures-in-gop-as-some-conservatives-embrace-renewable-energy.html?_r=0Seeking Alpha, 2015.

"California's New GHG Reduction Target Is a Huge Boon for the Solar Industry," *Seeking Alpha*. Online: http://seekingalpha.com/article/3121476-californias-new-ghg-reduction-target-is-a-huge-boon-for-the-solar-industry

Thich Nhat Hanh, *Fear: Essential Wisdom for Getting*

Through the Storm (New York: Harper, 2012) was of particular personal resonance for me. http://plumvillage.org/about/thich-nhat-hanh/.

Vandana Shiva, *Staying Alive: Women, Ecology and Development* (London: Zed Books 1989).

Vandava Shiva, *Making Peace with the Planet* (London: Pluto Press, 2012).

Siemens, 2015. Siemens highlights cost-cutting innovations for offshore wind at European trade show Hamburg, 2015-Feb-26 http://www.siemens.com/press/en/pressrelease/?press=/en/pressrelease/2015/windpowerrenewables/pr2015020140wpen.htm&content[]=WP&content[]=EM.

Suzzane W. Sinard, "The Foundational Role of Mycorrhizal Networks in Self-Organization of Interior Douglas-Fir Forests," *Forest Ecology and Management* (Elsevier: February 12, 2009).Online: http://www.cof.orst.edu/cof/teach/fs545/Readings/Simard 2009.pdf.

Skeptical Science, 2015. "CO2 does indeed appear to have a long atmospheric lifetime." *Skeptical Science.* Online: http://www.skepticalscience.com/co2-residence-time.htm.

Richard Schlesinger, "What's a Watt Worth?" *EnergyBiz Magazine,* Summer 2015.

Appy Sluijs , Mark Pagani, Henk Brinkhuis, Japp S. Sinninghe Damsté, Gerald R. Dickens, Martin Huber, Gert-Jan Reichart, Jens Matthiessen, Ruediger Stein,Lucas J. Lourens, Nikolai Pedentchouk, Jan Backman, Kathryn Moran, *2006.* "Subtropical Arctic Ocean temperatures during the Paleocene/Eocene thermal maximum," *Nature* 441, 610-613 (1 June 2006). http://www.nature.com/nature/journal/v441/n7093/full/nature04668.html\l"a3".

Source Watch. "Bangladesh and Coal."Online: http://www.sourcewatch.org/index.php/Bangladesh_and_coal.

Stanford Encyclopedia of Philosophy, "Biological Altruism (2003)." http://plato.stanford.edu/entries/altruism-biological/

State of Green, "Profile: City of Copenhagen (2015)." https://stateofgreen.com/en/profiles/city-of-copenhagen.

SolarCity, "SolarCity Introduces Affordable New Energy Storage Services Across the U.S." SolarCity. April 15, 2015. http://www.solarcity.com/newsroom/press/solarcity-introduces-affordable-new-energy-storage-services-across-us.

SolarCity, "SolarCity Activates Fund to Finance More Than $1 Billion in Commercial Solar Projects with Investment from Credit Suisse," SolarCity April 22, 2015. http://www.solarcity.com/newsroom/press/solarcity-activates-fund-finance-more-1-billion-commercial-solar-projects-investment.

Sundance Solar, Sunbender Do-it-Yourself Solar LED Jar Light Kit—Prewired, no soldering (2015). This system is being adapted for student assembly and sale. http://store.sundancesolar.com/sunbender-do-it-yourself-solar-led-jar-light-kit-pre-wired-no-soldering/

Tang Danlu, "Xinhua Insight: Discovering China's New, Normal Growth" (2014). http://news.xinhuanet.com/english/indepth/2014-10/03/c_133691531.

Herman K. Trabish, "New Vermont Law Mandates 75% Renewables by 2032, Targets Residential emissions." *Utility Dive* (2015).
http://www.utilitydive.com/news/new-vermont-law-mandates-75-renewables-by-2032-targets-residential-emissi/400777/.

Herman K. Trabish, "Co-op offers renewables only EV charging, highlighting new opportunity for utilities: Selling off-peak renewable kWhs to beat the rising cost of gasoline could also drive an EV boom," *Utility Dive* (2015).
http://www.utilitydive.com/news/co-op-offers-renewables-only-ev-charging-highlighting-new-opportunity-for/400779.

United Kingdom, Socialist Group 2008. "Global warming and ecological disasters." Parliamentary Assembly. Committee on the Environment, Agriculture and Local and Regional Affairs. Rapporteur: Mr. Alan Meale, United Kingdom, Socialist Group.
http://assembly.coe.int/ASP/Doc/XrefViewHTML.asp?FileID=11800&Language=EN

United Nations Department of Economic and Social Affairs (UNDESA), 2011. *World Economic and Social Survey 2011—The Great Green Technological Transformation, Chapter 2.*
http://www.un.org/en/development/desa/policy/wess/wess_current/2011wess_chapter2.pdf

U.S. Dept of Energy, 2012. "How Can A gallon of Gasoline Produce Twenty Pounds of Carbon Dioxide?"
http://www.fueleconomy.gov/feg/co2.shtml. Viewed Sept. 27, 2012.

U.S. Energy Information Agency, 2013. "Carbon Dioxide Emissions Coefficients." Online:
http://www.eia.gov/environment/emissions/co2_vol_mass.cfm.

U.S. Department of Energy, 2015. "All Electric Vehicles." U.S. Department of Energy.
http://www.fueleconomy.gov/feg/evtech.shtml.

Venus Project, "About the Venus Project" (2015).
https://www.thevenusproject.com/en/about/the-venus-project.

Vermont Public Service Department, *Total Energy Study* (Montpelier, Vermont, 2014).
http://publicservice.vermont.gov/sites/psd/files/Pubs_Plans_Reports/TES/TES%20FINAL%20Report%2020141208.pdf.

Ernst von Weizsacker, Ernst Ulrich, Charlie Hargroves, Michael H. Smith, Cheryl Desha, and Peter Stasinopoulos, *Factor Five: Transforming the Global Economy through 80% Improvements in Resource Productivity.* (Sterling, Virginia: Earth Scan, 2009).

Robert Wood, "BP Does Not Stand for Big Penalty," *Forbes,* July 3, 2017. http://www.forbes.com/sites/robertwood/2015/07/03/big-oil-spill-tax-write-off-shows-bp-does-not-stand-for-big-penalty/.

James Wight, 2011. "The Rapid Pulse of PETM CO2 Followed by Rapid Warming Indicates High Climate Sensitivity." *Skeptical Science.* June 7, 2011.
http://www.skepticalscience.com/christy-crock-6-climate-sensitivity.html.

Wetlands International, 2015. "Carbon Emissions from Peat Lands." Wetlands.org.
http://www.wetlands.org/Whatarewetlands/Peatlands/Carbonemissions-frompeatlands/tabid/2738/Default.aspx.

Michael P. Weinstein, R. Eugene Turner, & Carles Ibáñez, 2013. "The Global Sustainability transition: It Is More Than Changing Light Bulbs." *Sustainability, Practice & Politics.*
http://sspp.proquest.com/archives/vol9iss1/1203-005.weinstein.html.

Wikipedia, 2015, "States of India by Installed Power Capacity."
http://en.wikipedia.org/wiki/States_of_India_by_installed_power_capacity

World Bank, 2013, "Warming Climate to Hit Bangladesh Hard with Sea-Level Rise, More Floods and Cyclones, World Bank Report Says."
http://www.worldbank.org/en/news/press-release/2013/06/19/warming-climate-to-hit-bangladesh-hard-with-sea-level-rise-more-floods-and-cyclones-world-bank-report-say.

World Bank 2013, "Bolsa Família: Changing the Lives of Millions in Brazil."
http://web.worldbank.org/WBSITE/EXTERNAL/NEWS/0,content-MDK:21447054~pagePK:64257

World Bank 2015, "CO2 Emissions."
http://data.worldbank.org/indicator/EN.ATM.CO2E.PC

World Cultural Forum 2013, Hangzhou Declaration, 2013.
http://www.ciwg.net/hangzhou-declaration.html.

World Economic and Social Survey 2011. "Chapter II: The Clean Energy Technological Transformation." United Nations World Economic and Social Survey 2011.
http://www.un.org/en/development/desa/policy/wess/wess_current/2011wess_chapter2.pdf.

World Future Council 2015. "Japan's Top Runner Programme," Future Policy.org.
http://www.futurepolicy.org/ecologically-intelligent-design/japans-top-runner-programme

Worldwide-tax.com, 2012. "China V.A.T. and Other Taxes 2012."
http://www.worldwide-tax.com/china/chi_other.asp.
Viewed August 18, 2012.

Committee on Climate Change, 2015, "Carbon Budgets and Targets."
http://www.theccc.org.uk/tackling-climate-change/reducing-carbon-emissions/carbon-budgets-and-targets/.

Yale Project on Climate Change Communication, 2015. "Not All Republicans Think Alike on Global Warming." (*Yale School of Forestry*).
http://environment.yale.edu/climate-communication/article/not-all-republicans-think-alike-about-global-warming/#sthash.rCEtQ7IK.dpuf.

Xu Yan, "China's VAT Experience" in *The VAT Reader* (Arlington, VA: Tax Analysts, 2011), p. 322.
http://www.taxanalysts.com/www/freefiles.nsf/Files/YAN-25.pdf/$-file/YAN-25.pdf.

Xu Yan, "China adds 3.32 GW of Solar Capacity in HI," Xinhua (2014).
http://news.xinhuanet.com/english/china/2014-08/08/c_133540443.

Yang Li, "Wind Power Capacity Near China Development Target," Xinhua, 2014.
http://news.xinhuanet.com/english/china/2014-10/22/c_133734929.

Yang Li, "Chinese Statisticians Broaden Focus from GDP," Xinhua, 2014.
http://news.xinhuanet.com/english/china/2014-09/12/c_133638734.

Yaneer Bar-Yam, "Concepts: Emergence," New England ComplexSystems Institute (2011)
http://necsi.edu/guide/concepts/emergence.html.

Zhang Chun, 2015. "Civil Society Call for China-led Development Bank to Foster Green Growth." *China Dialogue*. Online: https://www.chinadialogue.net/blog/7878-Civil-society-call-for-China-led-development-bank-to-foster-green-growth/en.

Florian Zickfeld, Aglaia Wieland, et al., *Desert Power 2050: Executive Summary, The Case for Desert Power*. Dii Gmbh: Kaiserstr. 14 80801, Munich. June 2012. http://www.dii-eumena.com/fileadmin/flippingbooks/dp2050_exec_sum_engl_web.pdf.

Index

F

About the Author

Photo by Luanne Baker

ROY MORRISON is a writer and energy consultant with over thirty years of diverse experience. He has extensive experience in energy efficiency work, performing energy audits and technical assistance analysis for business, institutional, and government clients. He was the author of the first law in the nation for municipal aggregation for retail electric competition. He also founded the New Hampshire Consumers Utility Cooperative that was the first seller of competitive electricity in New Hampshire. He was a founding staff member of the University of New Hampshire Energy Office.

Roy Morrison was Founding Director of the Office for Sustainability at Southern New Hampshire University. He has worked on the development of renewable energy hedges, Advanced Energy Performance Contracting for market-based mass retrofits of efficiency and renewables, and renewable Super Grid development.

He is currently working on building solar farms in several states with a focus on using rooftops and marginal and contaminated land to be restored for productive energy use. He pursues a variety of sustainability initiatives, including zero carbon planning and greenhouse gas mitigation and adaptation planning for New England towns and cities.

He delivered a plenary address at the 2013 World Social Forum in Hangzhou, which issued the Hangzhou declaration calling for global development of an ecological civilization. Chinese colleagues report he was the first person globally to discuss an ecological civilization in his book *Ecological Investigations.* He recently edited Xinhua News Agency Los Angeles Bureau's China Ecological Civilization Annual Report and Outlook 2014-2015 and has written op-eds for the *Beijing's People's Daily* assessing China's ecological improvement progress and opportunities for leadership at the Paris 2015 United Nations Climate Conference.

Roy Morrison's energy work and social theory books were a logical consequence of his safe-energy and antinuclear activism. He was an organizer and safe-energy activist with the Clamshell Alliance in the 1970s and 1980s, cofounder of the American Peace Test, and staff for the Nuclear Freeze Campaign in the 1980s. He helped organize and participated in many large and small nonviolent direct actions, often risking arrest, in support of safe energy and nuclear disarmament, and in opposition to nuclear power and nuclear weapons testing.

Roy Morrison is a kayaker, and with his wife, Luanne Baker Morrison, he walks 1,000 miles a year—5,376 miles so far since March 2010.

His son, Sam Schaffer-Morrison, age 22, is studying conservation biology and currently works at Barro Colorado Smithsonian tropical research station in Panama.

He is the author of numerous books, including *Ecological Civilization 2140: A 22nd Century History and Survivor's Journal,* and a book of poetry called *The Loggers of Warner.*

For more information about Morrison's recent work, please visit: http://www.ecocivilizationweebly.com/

For information about his publications, please visit his Amazon book page: http://www.amazon.com/Roy-Morrison/e/B000APW44U